Rills from the Fountain of Life

Frontispiece. RILLS FROM THE FOUNTAIN OF LIFE.

RILLS

FROM

THE FOUNTAIN OF LIFE

OR

GOOD WORDS FOR THE YOUNG

BY

REV. RICHARD NEWTON, D.D.

AUTHOR OF "THE BEST THINGS," "BIBLE BLESSINGS,"
"BIBLE JEWELS," "BIBLE WONDERS," ETC.

SOLID GROUND CHRISTIAN BOOKS
PORT ST LUCIE, FLORIDA USA

SOLID GROUND CHRISTIAN BOOKS
1682 SW PANCOAST STREET
PORT ST LUCIE, FL 34987
205-587-4480
www.solid-ground-books.com
mike.sgcb@gmail.com

RILLS FROM THE FOUNTAIN OF LIFE
or Good Words for the Young

By Richard Newton (1813-1887)

First Solid Ground Edition April 2018

Taken from 1880 edition by William P. Nimmo & Co
Edinburgh, Scotland

Cover Design by Borgo Design, Tuscaloosa, Alabama

ISBN: 978-159925-3817

CONTENTS.

	PAGE
THE PLEASANT WAY	1
THE SPIDER'S EXAMPLE	16
THE MARKS OF A BEN-ONI	30
THE CROOKED THINGS STRAIGHTENED	51
THE GREAT MAN IN GOD'S SIGHT	62
THE LILY'S LESSONS	76
THE GIFT FOR GOD	88
THE WONDERFUL LAMP	98
THE CHILD'S FORTUNE TOLD	110
THE MILLENNIAL MENAGERIE	123
THE BEST MERCHANDISE	137
THE LESSONS JESUS TEACHES	148

TO

The Sunday-School Teachers

OF

ST. PAUL'S CHURCH,

IN TESTIMONY OF
THEIR EARNEST AND HEARTY CO-OPERATION WITH HIM IN EVERY GOOD WORK
AND OF THE DEGREE IN WHICH
THEIR CHEERFUL, AND HARMONIOUS AID HAS HELPED
TO SWEETEN THE CARES, AND LIGHTEN THE BURDENS, OF SIXTEEN YEARS
OF MINISTERIAL LABOUR AMONG THEM,

This Little Volume

IS RESPECTFULLY DEDICATED, BY THEIR AFFECTIONATE

FRIEND AND PASTOR.

PREFACE.

The following sermons have been published at the request of the teachers of the Sunday-schools of St. Paul's Church. For the ast two years, there has been a service for the children of t is congregation, on the afternoon of the first Sunday in tl . month. On these occasions, the children occupy the bod· of the church. The usual service is performed, and a se rmon preached, designed especially for the benefit of the children.

It is called, "*The Children's Church.*" It was begun, at first, with much doubt and fear, as a matter of experiment. The result has proved, in the highest degree, satisfactory and encouraging. The children have manifested the liveliest interest in these services. In reply to questions asked, they always give an intelligent account of the outlines of the last sermon preached. The adult attendance, on these occasions, is larger than at any other afternoon service in this church. While the preacher has found the effort at arrangement, and simplification, necessary in order to secure the attention of so youthful an auditory, of great profit to himself, in sermonizing for "children of a larger growth."

This little volume contains a portion of the sermons delivered on these occasions. They were preached extemporaneously, and written out, from the original notes, during the last summer vacation. It was the opinion of the teachers who heard them, that, as they had interested the children of one school, they might be useful to others. And, in compliance with their earnest and united request, this unpretending little offering is laid upon the altar of the Sunday-school cause, with the fervent prayer, that, *that* glorious Saviour who hath "chosen the weak things of the world to confound the things that are mighty;" and whose sacred, standing, injunction to his ministers is, *"Feed my lambs,"* may graciously crown it with his blessing, and make it an humble instrument of good to some of his "little ones."

RILLS FROM THE FOUNTAIN.

THE PLEASANT WAY.

" Her ways are ways of pleasantness, and all her paths are peace."—Prov. iii. 7.

THE question any one feels tempted to ask on reading these words is, *Whose* ways are here spoken of? Now, if we look at the thirteenth verse of this chapter, we find that the person intended here is Wisdom. In the Bible, when Wisdom is spoken of as a person, it always means true Religion. And so we find that it is Religion of which Solomon is speaking when he says, " *Her* ways are ways of pleasantness," &c.

The Bible tells us of *two* great roads or ways in which the people of this world are walking. One of these is the world's way, or the way of sin; the other is Wisdom's way, or the way of Religion. One of these is called the *broad* way, and multitudes are always thronging it; the other is called the narrow way, and but few are found to travel it. In the language of the hymn,—

> " Broad is the road that leads to death,
> And thousands walk together there;
> But Wisdom shows a narrow path,
> With here and there a traveller."

Now, there are *six* things which help to make a road

pleasant to those who travel it, and all these are found in Wisdom's ways.

The first thing which makes a way pleasant is to have a SAFE GUIDE.

If you had to journey through a country in which there were no roads laid out, it would be very unpleasant; because you would never be able to tell, with any certainty, whether you were going right or not. When ships are at sea, they find no roads laid out over the broad surface of its waters. There are no milestones to mark the distance, and no finger-boards to point out the way. But the sailor takes the compass, with its little trembling needle always pointing to the north, and this becomes his guide. This enables him to tell which way to go. This is just as good to him as roads and finger-boards. The sailor's way at sea would be a very unpleasant one if he had no compass as his guide. But the guidance which this gives him does much to make his way a way of pleasantness.

Near the city of Rome, in Italy, there is an extensive burial-place, called the Catacombs. It is all under ground, and reaches for miles in different ways. The paths, among the tombs, cross each other in every possible direction, so that even in the broad light of day it would be a perfect puzzle to find one's way through them. But no ray of light reaches that gloomy place. It is dark as midnight there. Of course, then, you will easily understand that to enter the Catacombs without a guide is a very dangerous thing. So many lives have been lost, in consequence, that the entrances have been closed up, and no persons are now permitted to go in. Before this was done, however, there was once a young man who resolved to explore the Catacombs. He furnished himself with a light, and, in order that he might not lose his way, he took a ball of string, and, fastening one end of it at the entrance of the dark passage, he carried the ball with him that he might guide his way out by it. Having thus furnished himself, he went in, and trod cautiously along, gazing in silence on the different names and memorials inscribed on the tombs in that dark city of the dead. He spent some hours in this manner; and, dark and dismal as the place was, his way was comparatively pleasant, because he had a guide. But when he was about turning to go back his light went out. And in the alarm which this threw him into, he dropped his string, which was all he had to depend on to lead him back to the outside world of light and life. He stooped down at once to pick up his guiding-string, but he could not find it. He got down on his knees, and felt carefully around in every direction for that precious, precious thread, on which hung all his hope of life and deliverance; but in vain. He turned and groped, and groped and turned, till weary with the effort; but to no purpose. Then he began to despair. He felt that he was buried alive. He thought of his home, of his friends, and of the bright and beautiful world without, and wept bitter tears of sorrow over his folly in entering that gloomy abode. But he soon felt that weeping would do him no good. So he resolved to make a desperate effort to escape, before giving himself up to die. Then he began in utter darkness to grope his way back. But he had no guide; and, ah! he felt how dreadfully unpleasant his way was made simply by his want of a guide. He walked on in darkness till compelled to stop and rest. Again he walked, and again he rested. He continued his efforts for hours, that seemed like ages to him. But it was for life that he was struggling, and so he toiled on, and on, and on, till at last his energies were exhausted. He felt that it was of no use. He thought that he must die; and, just as he was sinking in utter despair to the earth, he thought he saw a faint glimmer of light. This revived his sinking heart. He struggled on a little farther; he turned a corner of the way; and, oh, joy of joys to him! there was the broad light of day. A merciful Providence had directed his steps in the dark and brought him out in safety.

A *safe guide* is the first thing necessary to make a way pleasant. In Religion's way we have this. The *Bible* is our guide here. It is a safe guide. It never leads us wrong. It shows us the dangers in our path, and how we may avoid them. It will go with us all through life, and lead us to heaven at last. Religion's ways are ways of pleasantness, because we have a safe guide in these ways.

But *the second thing which makes a way pleasant is* GOOD COMPANY.

If you have a journey to take all alone, with no one to talk to on the way, how long and dreary that journey will seem! But if you have two or three friends and companions with you, whom you love very much, and they talk with you as you travel on, telling you all about the different houses you pass by, the names and characters of the people who live in them, and all about the different places that come in sight, and the various things that have happened in connection with them, this will keep your mind fully occupied. You would not feel tired; the time would pass without your knowing it, and the way would seem very short, and very pleasant. Now, those who walk in Wisdom's ways have the very best company. All good Christians are their fellow-travellers. You remember how Moses spoke to his father-in-law, when he wanted to persuade him to become an Israelite, and serve God with him and his people. He said (Numb. x. 29), "Come thou with us, and we will do thee good; for we are journeying to the place of which the Lord hath said, I will give you."

And so, when we begin to serve God, we are travelling to the land of promise, the heavenly Canaan, the good land which God will give to His people. And Wisdom's ways are the ways in which we are to travel to reach that land. And all God's people are our fellow-travellers, in trying to reach that happy land. But we have *better* company than this in Wisdom's ways. The holy angels are the companions of all who walk in these ways. St Paul says that the angels "are all ministering spirits, sent forth to minister unto those who are heirs of salvation." This means all true Christians,—all who love and serve God.

THE BEST COMPANY. 5

And David says, "The angel of the Lord encampeth round about them that fear Him, and delivereth them."

Now, these angels are *silent* companions: they are not allowed to speak to us. They are *invisible* companions: we cannot see them. But still they are *real* companions of all who walk in Wisdom's ways. But, though silent and invisible, they are active and useful companions. God employs them to take care of us, to protect us from harm, and prevent many evils that Satan and his evil spirits would inflict upon us.

But we have better company even than this in Wisdom's ways. God Himself will be the companion of all who walk in these ways. Enoch walked in these ways, before the flood; and when the Bible tells us about him, it says, "Enoch walked with God." And if Enoch walked with God, then God must have walked with Enoch. Jesus says, "If a man love me, he will keep my words; and my Father will love him, and we will come unto him, *and make our abode with him.*" And St Paul says, "Truly our fellowship,"—and fellowship, you know, is just the same as companionship,—"our fellowship is with the Father and with His Son Jesus Christ." Ah! this is good company indeed; this is the very best company we can have. Only think, my dear children, of having the Lord Jesus Christ for a companion! And though He is invisible too, like the angels, yet He is not silent too, like them. Oh, no; He *speaks* to His people as He walks with them, and what He says makes them very happy. As He walked with His disciples when on earth, and talked with them, on one occasion, "their hearts burned within them," and they were so happy they hardly knew what to do. And just so He talks with His people now. It is not, indeed, by words, spoken to their outward ears, that Jesus talks with His people now, but by thoughts put into their minds by His Holy Spirit. In this way He speaks to them of the precious promises of His Word, of what He has done and suffered for their salvation, and of the glorious home which He has prepared for them above. There is nothing in the world can make us so happy as to have Jesus for our companion. A good man, who loved Jesus very much, once wrote a beautiful hymn about the happiness he found in the companionship of Jesus; and in that hymn he says,—

> "While blest with a sense of His love,
> A palace a toy would appear;
> And prisons would palaces prove
> If Jesus would dwell with me there."

The good company found in Wisdom's ways is the second thing which makes them "ways of pleasantness."

The third thing which makes a way pleasant is SURE PROTECTION.

If you were walking along a road in which steel-traps were hidden, and you were in danger, at every step, of being caught in them, there would be no pleasantness in that way. The danger would take away all pleasure. You remember our Saviour told a story once about a man who went down from Jerusalem to Jericho, and fell among thieves, who robbed, and stripped, and wounded him, and left him half dead. The road from Jerusalem to Jericho was a very dangerous road then. It was a narrow road that ran winding round between high mountains. There were dark caverns in the sides of the mountains. These caverns were infested with robbers, who watched for the passing travellers, and sprang out to rob and murder them. That road is just as dangerous now as it was then. So many murders have been committed there that it is called "the bloody way." There would be no pleasantness in travelling that way. There would be no *safety*, even, unless you had a company of armed men to protect you. *Protection*, in travelling, is necessary if we would have pleasure in it.

Now, the way of life through which we are travelling is a way full of dangers. Like the road from Jerusalem to Jericho, it is beset with robbers. Satan, with his evil spirits, is there, like the captain of a band of robbers. His object is to rob our souls of all right feelings and prin-

THE DANGEROUS WAY.

ciples, and drag us down to his own dark den for ever. He is the worst robber that ever was. There is nothing we should dread so much as falling into his hands, and being left there. Yet this must happen to all who do not walk in Wisdom's ways. We cannot protect ourselves against this robber. Our best friends and dearest relations cannot protect us. Jesus alone can afford us protection here. *We* cannot *see* Satan, but *He* can. We know not where he lays his traps and snares for us, but Jesus knows. And He can turn away our feet and keep us from falling into those snares. He said to Abraham once, when he was in danger, "Fear not, Abraham; I am thy *shield*." Abraham was travelling the same way of life that we are travelling. He was exposed to the same dangers from Satan's power and malice that we are exposed to. Protection from this danger was necessary for him, in order that he might find pleasantness in that way. And Jesus promised to be his shield, and assured him of this protection. And this promise belongs to you and me, if we walk in Wisdom's ways, as much as it did to Abraham. Jesus will give us sure protection from Satan, the great robber of souls. Do you ask, How will Jesus protect us? Let me tell you. In the sixth chapter of the Second Book of Kings we find a very interesting story of the prophet Elisha. He was living in a little village on a mountain in Israel. The king of Syria was at war with the king of Israel at that time. And whenever the Syrian king held a secret council with the captains of his army, and laid a plan for making a sudden attack upon the Israelites, Elisha knew it by the spirit of prophecy, and sent word to the king of Israel, who went there with his army, and prevented the attack of the Syrians. This made the king of Syria very angry; and he sent an army of soldiers to take the prophet prisoner and put him to death. This army came by night, and, finding out the place of Elisha's abode, they quite surrounded the mountain, and filled the lower part of it with their numbers. When the prophet's servant arose in the morning, and saw how they were surrounded by the horses and chariots of their enemies, he was greatly afraid, and cried out, "Alas! my master, what shall we do?" But Elisha felt no fear. He knew very well what safe protection they had, and he wanted his servant to know it too. Then he prayed that God would give his servant power to see what he saw, and God opened his eyes to see spiritual beings; and, oh! what a sight did he behold! How it must have amazed him! He saw the mountain full of horses and chariots of fire round his master and himself. These were angels that God had sent to take care of them. What harm could the Syrians do them while they had such a guard? None at all. No wonder, then, that Elisha was not hurt, but was saved in the singular way described in the chapter which tells this interesting story. This shows us what a wonderful shield God is to His people, and how He can protect them from Satan and his hosts, just as easily as He protected Elisha from the army of the Syrians. Here we see how true the language of that hymn is which says,—

> "That man no guard nor weapon needs
> Whose heart the blood of Jesus knows;
> But safe may pass, when duty leads,
> Through burning sands or mountain-snows.
>
> "Released from guilt, he feels no fear;
> Redemption is his shield and tower;
> He sees his Saviour always near
> To help in every trying hour.
>
> "His love possessing, I am blest,
> Secure, whatever change may come;
> Whether I go to east or west,
> With Him I still shall be at home."

Yes, yes, dear children, there is *sure protection* to those who walk in Wisdom's ways; and this makes up part of the pleasantness which is found in those ways.

But there is a fourth thing which tends to make travelling pleasant in any way; and that is, to have PROPER PROVISION *made for our wants.*

Every person who has ever had to travel all day, and carry a burden, will understand what a very pleasant thing it is to get to a good stopping-place at night. To be able to set down your burden, and wash away the dust and soil of a weary journey; and then to have a good substantial supper provided, and, after satisfying your hunger, to have a nice, clean, comfortable bed to rest in :—these are the things which travellers want, and it is having *proper provision* made to supply these wants which imparts pleasantness to their ways. Where this provision has not been made, or cannot be obtained, there can be no pleasure in travelling. We often hear of sailors, far off at sea, who run short of food and water. Their provisions fail; they have nothing to eat or drink, and it is impossible for them to get any. Ah! there is very little pleasantness in the sailor's way then. Starvation and suffering stare him in the face, but he cannot help himself.

And travellers on land, as well as on the sea, at times, find provisions fail them, and then what terrible unpleasantness is felt in their ways! Some time ago a company was fitted out from a United States naval vessel, under the command of Lieutenant Strain, to explore the Isthmus of Darien, and see if it would be possible to make a canal across it, so that vessels might get from the Atlantic to the Pacific Ocean without having to go all the way round South America and Cape Horn. They expected to get through and be back again in a few days, and only took provisions with them accordingly. But they found the distance many times greater than it had been represented to them. They had to make their toilsome way through a trackless, tangled wilderness. It took them about as many weeks as they expected to be days employed upon it. Their provisions entirely failed. They would toil all day on their painful journey, and then have nothing to eat at night but such roots, or berries, or nuts as they might gather on their way. Their way was a way of unpleasantness, because they had no *proper provision* for their wants. Some of them died of starvation, and they were all wasted away to mere skeletons before they got through. The officers and men engaged in that expedition displayed a degree of brave endurance and nobleness of character which was perhaps never exceeded, and which reflects the highest honour on themselves and on their country. And *they* would understand, much better than we can, how greatly the pleasantness of travellers' ways depends on having a proper provision for their wants. But those who walk in Wisdom's ways have a provision for their wants that never fails. The Bible says to them, "God will supply all you need, out of the riches of His grace, in Christ Jesus." God's Sabbaths are the resting-days which He has appointed for the refreshment of those who are travelling in Wisdom's ways. The church is like an inn, which He has fitted and furnished for their comfort. Here a constant feast is prepared for them. Here is the bread which came down from heaven, and of which whosoever eateth shall live for ever. Here are the wells of salvation, from which His people draw water with great joy. It is living water which they yield. Those who drink of this water never thirst again, but they carry it with them, "a well of water, springing up unto everlasting life." When David was walking in these ways he said, "The Lord is my Shepherd; I shall not want. He maketh me to lie down in green pastures; He leadeth me beside the still waters." In another place he says that others "may lack and suffer hunger, but they that wait upon the Lord" —and this means those who walk in Wisdom's ways— "shall want *no manner of thing that is good*." *That* is a glorious promise indeed; and it is a precious provision which it makes for all who are walking in Wisdom's ways. Truly there is a proper provision for them, and this makes the ways in which they are walking "ways of pleasantness."

But there is a fifth thing which helps to make a way pleasant, and that is a PLEASANT PROSPECT.

Everybody, I suppose, has heard of the great desert of Sahara in Africa. It reaches for hundreds of miles, in

A VIEW IN SWITZERLAND.—*Rills from the Fountain of Life*, p. 11.

every direction, like a vast ocean of sand. There are no roads, no shady resting-places, nor cool fountains, there. No tall dark mountains there lift up their huge forms to the view. No fields of grain, no valleys thick with corn, no murmuring brooks, no flowery gardens, no beautiful groves, are there. Go where you will, turn where you may, wide wastes of barren, burning sands are all the eye can rest upon. Suppose we had to travel, day after day, over those dreary desert sands: would there be much pleasantness in our way? No, indeed. The want of a pleasant prospect would make it as uncomfortable as it well could be. We should be all the time thinking about some of the beautiful roads we had travelled in our own country, like the shady lanes about Germantown, or that most charming road along the Wissahickon; and the remembrance of them would make the desert seem gloomier still by contrast. Switzerland, you know, is a country famous, all over the world, for its beautiful scenery. Hundreds and thousands of people go there every year, just for the purpose of admiring its beauties. And those who travel through that country find their ways made ways of pleasantness, simply by the *pleasant prospects* which are before them there. They see mountains whose tops are covered with snow. Sometimes the clouds gather round them, and then, again, the sunbeams are reflected from them in all the varying colours of the rainbow. Other mountains are seen clothed with dark green woods, and streams of water are gushing down their sides like threads of silver, and wild torrents dash themselves into foam and spray. The prospect varies and changes continually, and affords unceasing pleasantness to those whose ways lead them through that land of beauty.

But now you may be ready to ask, What sort of prospects are afforded to those who walk in Wisdom's ways? Oh, here are pleasant prospects indeed! Nothing in all the world can be compared to these for interest and beauty. Prospects of heaven are to be seen from these ways. Did you ever read Bunyan's "Pilgrim's Progress?" Next to the Bible, it is one of the best books in the world. Everybody ought to read it. It represents the Christian, in one part of his journey, as reaching an elevated region called "the Delectable Mountains," and looking through a telescope, and getting a view of heaven. Now, there are many of these mountains in Wisdom's ways, and heaven can be clearly seen from the top of them. The promises which God has written in the Bible are what I mean by these mountains. Look, for instance, at the last two chapters of the book of the Revelation: what a beautiful description of heaven we have there! Why, when we read those chapters we feel as if we were standing on the top of a high mountain, and having a prospect of heaven, in all its glory, spread out before us. That is the fullest and clearest prospect of it that we have. But there are a great many other prospects of heaven to be met with in Wisdom's ways, less clear and extensive than this, yet all beautiful and pleasant prospects. And the writer of that sweet hymn which we sometimes sing had been looking at these prospects, or meditating on the promises of God's Word, when he wrote,—

> "There is a land of pure delight,
> Where saints immortal reign;
> Eternal day excludes the night,
> And pleasures banish pain.
>
> "There everlasting spring abides,
> And never-fading flowers:
> Death, like a narrow sea, divides
> This heavenly land from ours.
>
> "Bright fields, beyond the swelling flood,
> Stand dressed in living green;
> So, to the Jews, fair Canaan stood,
> While Jordan rolled between."

And these *pleasant prospects*, found in Wisdom's ways, make them ways of pleasantness.

There is only one other thing I would speak of as making a way pleasant, and that is, to have A COMFORTABLE END *in view.*

A COMFORTABLE END.

When we are taking a journey, the question, Where are we going? must have a great effect upon our feelings. Every boy or girl who has had to go from home to boarding-school will understand all about this. You remember how different your feelings were, when you were going away from home, from what they were when you were returning home. Yet it was the same way that you travelled in both cases. The chief thing which made the difference was the *end* you had in view. On first taking that journey, you knew that the end of it was a school among strangers. You were going to mingle with persons whom you had never seen or known before. You were going to engage in duties that were new and trying. You expected to meet with difficulties and perplexities in this new situation, and you knew not yet what these would be. But you were afraid of them, and the mere thought of them was enough to make you feel uncomfortable. The end in view made your way unpleasant. But, ah! how different it was when vacation-time came, and you were leaving school! The road you had to travel was the same, but the end in view was different, and that made, oh, what a change in your feelings! Instead of school, with its strange faces and hard duties, you had now nothing to think of but your dear, sweet, happy home, with the looks of love, and smiles of affection, and all the fond familiar objects which you knew were awaiting you there. And the thought of these things—the *comfortable end* you had in view—made your way home a way of unmingled pleasantness. And it is just the same in any other journey. Here, for example, is a stage-coach just starting on a journey of a hundred miles. Among the passengers are two young men. They are both going to the same place. They are going by the same road; they are in the same conveyance, sitting on the same seat; they eat the same food; they breathe the same air; they look out on the same beautiful scenery; and yet, while one of them talks, and smiles, and looks bright and happy as a summer morning, the other looks very differently.

He speaks to no one. He never smiles. He takes no notice of the beautiful country; but, with downcast eye and melancholy looks, he tries to avoid the observation of those about him, and seems like the image of sorrow and despair. The way they are travelling is a way of pleasantness to one of these young men, but a way of gloom and sadness to the other. And what makes the difference? It is the *end* they have in view. One of them has been travelling in Europe for several years, and is now returning to the home of his childhood. His family and friends are all eagerly expecting him, and ready, with open arms, and warm, affectionate hearts, to welcome him back again. His heart is fairly dancing within him, and every nerve in his system is tingling with delight. He has a comfortable end in view, and *that* makes his way all pleasantness. But the other,—poor fellow!—he has committed a forgery. His crime has been found out. He has been taken up, and is now on his way back to be tried, condemned, and punished. The grief and sorrow of his family and friends, and a prison with its deep and enduring disgrace,—this is the end before him: and can you wonder that it makes his way a way of unpleasantness?

And the end we have in view in the great journey of life has just the same effect upon our feelings. Those who are walking in Wisdom's ways have a very comfortable end in view. They have a glorious home in heaven to look forward to. *There*, in the company of all good people, with the holy angels, and God their Father, and Jesus their blessed Saviour, they shall dwell for ever in unspeakable happiness. Oh, this is a comfortable end to have in view! This cannot fail to make the ways of Wisdom pleasantness to those who walk in them. And when you think of these six things—*the safe guide, the good company, the sure protection, the proper provision, the pleasant prospect, and the comfortable end*—which are found in Wisdom's ways, you cannot wonder to hear it said that "her ways are ways of pleasantness."

And now I think I hear some of you asking, How can we get into these ways and walk in them? Let me tell you in a few closing words. When Jesus was on earth, He said, "*I am the way.*" At another time He said, "I am the door; by me, if any man enter in, he shall be saved." Now, we learn from these words that Wisdom's ways are all in Jesus; and the door of entrance into these ways is found in Jesus. If any one feels that he is a sinner, and wants to get his sins pardoned, he must go and pray to God to pardon his sins for Jesus' sake. If any one feels that his heart is wicked, and he cannot make it any better, he must go and pray to God for Jesus' sake to change his wicked heart, and take away all his wrong feelings, and make him like Jesus. We must read the Bible to find out what Jesus did, and what He has told us to do, and then pray to God to give us grace to do these things; and then we shall be walking in Wisdom's ways, and shall know ourselves how pleasant those ways are.

May God guide us all in these pleasant ways, and bring us to His Heavenly home at last, for Jesus' sake! Amen.

THE SPIDER'S EXAMPLE.

" The spider taketh hold with her hands, and is in kings' palaces."—PROV. xxx. 28.

Now, I dare say, my dear children, some of you will be ready to cry out, "What! going to speak about an ugly spider?" Yes, I am going to speak about the spider. I know we dislike spiders very much. Almost everybody dislikes them. Some run away from them as soon as they see them. Others try to kill them whenever they can. But although they are thus disliked and killed, there is a great deal to admire about the spider, and there is something which we should do well to imitate, too. Why, one of the prettiest things I ever remember to have seen was a spider's claw, when looked at through a microscope. Now, suppose we had a large microscope here. We catch a big spider and put him in, so that we may examine him carefully. Oh, there are some rare things for us now to see! When we put the crawler in, he was about as big as a bean; but see, now, there he is, almost as big as a bear. See, he is covered all over with rich, soft-looking fur. There is his huge head; and count how many eyes are in it. One, two, three, four, five, six, seven, eight! Yes, there are eight eyes in his head, as shining and bright as diamonds. Look, now, at his long legs. Each of them has a sort of hand at the end of it, with two fingers and a thumb. I suppose Solomon never saw a microscope, and never looked at a spider through one. Yet he knew what he was saying

WONDERFUL SPINNING-MACHINE.

when he spoke of it as taking hold with its "*hands,*" and not with its claws. But let us take one more look, through the microscope, at our spider. Right in the middle of his body is a curious spinning-machine. No human mechanic ever invented anything to compare with it. It weaves threads so delicate that the finest silk thread man ever wove seems almost like a *cable* in comparison with it. And yet each one of these very fine threads which the spider weaves is made up of *five thousand* different threads. What a wonderful spinning-machine is this! How little people think, when they thoughtlessly crush what they call "an ugly spider," how much that is curious, and wonderful, and really beautiful, they are crushing!

But you may ask, Well, what has all this to do with a Sunday-school sermon? Why, it has a good deal to do with it, as we shall see before we get through. Now, there are *three* questions which I am going to ask and answer; and these will be the things about this sermon which I want you especially to remember.

The first question is this:—What is there about the spider which it is worth our while to imitate?

The second is this:—What does the spider gain for itself by these things?

And the third is this:—What may we gain to ourselves by imitating these things?

Now, tell me the first question to be answered. What is there about the spider which it is worth our while to imitate? There are *two* things in the spider that we shall do well to imitate; and these are its *industry* and its *perseverance*. What are they? Industry means a love of work. The spider loves to work. It is born with a love of work. As soon as it begins to live it begins to work. Every spider is a weaver and a rigger. And the youngest spider knows how to do these things just as well as the oldest. The spider never has to go to school, or to take any lessons, in order to learn these trades. It knows them by what we call *instinct*. Instinct means the knowledge which God gives to animals and living creatures when He makes them. The little duck knows how to swim as soon as it is hatched, without any teaching. And so the little bird knows how to build its nest, and the bee to gather honey and make the honeycomb, without ever receiving a single lesson. God is the teacher of these creatures. He makes them understand how to do their work. And they always do it in the very best way. Not all the weavers, and spinners, and riggers in the world can beat the spider in the work that he does. Look at that broken window-pane, or at the upper corner of that doorway. The spider has been there, weaving his net. How light it is! It seems as though the least puff of wind would blow it away. But no; the strongest winds sweep by it, and yet it stands there still. See how regularly and straightly the threads are drawn, and see, too, how neatly the cross-pieces are fastened to them! The spider never does his work hurriedly and carelessly, as many children do. He always takes time for it, and does it well. His fastenings never come undone. He is really industrious and loves his work. Spiders have many different kinds of work to do, but they are all done in the very best manner. Some are hunting spiders. They spread their nets, just as the hunters set their traps, in the woods or fields, and wait patiently till their prey is caught in it, and then pounce upon them and devour them. Some are *mason*-spiders. These build little huts or houses, rather bigger than a thimble, to live in. They make doors to them, which they shut to when they go in, and even have something like bolts to fasten them with, so that they can keep robbers from entering. And then there is another kind of spider,—the fishing or diving spider. These live beside the water. They make a sort of waterproof house or diving-bell. In this they sink down to the bottom of the water, where they eat their food, and stay as long as they want to; and when they get hungry or tired of staying there, they come up to the top to enjoy a change of scene and get a fresh supply of provisions. And sometimes the spider seems to act just as if he had the power to reason, as men do. A gentleman who was very fond of studying the habits of different animals and insects, one day, when he was walking in his garden, found a large spider. It was near a pond of water. He took a long stick, and put the spider on one end of it. Then he went to the side of the pond, and, stretching out as far as he could, he thrust the other end of the stick down into the bottom of the pond, and left it standing straight up out of the water, with the spider upon it. He then sat down on the bank to watch what the spider would do when he found himself a prisoner there. Presently the spider began to move. First he went down the stick till he came to the water. He went round and round the stick, feeling and looking carefully, till he found there was no getting off there. Then he went to the top, and found there was no way of escape there. Then he went up and down the different sides of the stick, till he became satisfied that there was nothing leading from the stick by means of which he could possibly get away. Then he went once more to the top of the stick and remained quiet for a while. It seemed to the gentleman as though the spider were saying to himself, "Well, I'm in a nice fix now; what in the world am I to do?" He seemed to be taking observations from the top of the stick, making up his mind what he was to do next. Then he set the spinning-machine that he carried with him in operation. He wove out a long coil of thread,—long enough to reach to the shore from his island-prison. When he had done this he fastened one end of his thread to the top of the stick, and let the rest of it float in the breeze. When he had done this he went sliding down along the thread which he had spun till he reached the end, where, after floating in the air a little while, he lighted safely on the land and scampered away to his home. Now, certainly these things show us that the spider, notwithstanding his ugliness, deserves our respect. As an example of *industry* he is worthy of our imitation. Industry is a most honourable quality. It is becoming to those who occupy the humblest position in life, and it is equally becoming to those who occupy the highest position. When God made Adam and Eve, He put them in a garden that they might have an opportunity of being industrious, by dressing and keeping it, because He knew they could not be happy without industry, even in Paradise. For this same reason the angels are industrious in heaven. They serve God day and night. And they are very happy in serving Him. The greatest men have generally been the most industrious. Peter the Great, the Emperor of Russia, was a very remarkable man. He did more, perhaps, for the honour and welfare of his country than any other monarch that ever reigned over it. But all the greatness he gained for himself, and all the good he did for his country, was owing to his wonderful industry. He travelled from country to country, and learned, by working with his own hands, the different trades which he wanted to have introduced among his own people. And our own great and good Washington was as remarkable for his industry as he was for every excellence that could adorn a man, a general, or a ruler. On one occasion, during the Revolutionary War, he was going round, in disguise, to visit some log-forts that were being built. In the course of his walk he met with a company of men who were hard at work, under the command of a corporal. This petty officer, proud of his elevation above the common soldiers, was walking about, full of the thought of his own importance, and crying out every now and then, "Come! work away, boys!" but he never offered to help them. But Washington, when he saw that the men had more work than they could well do, took off his coat at once and began to help them, saying, "Spring to it, my brave fellows! we are working for our country; let us do it with a good will." He worked away with them till they got through; and then, when he was putting on his coat, he asked the officer why he did not help the men when he saw they had more work than they could well do. "I would have you to know, sir," said the *little* man, "that I am a corporal; I don't work!" "Oh! are you, sir?" said the *great* man; "I would have you to know that I am the commander-in-chief, and I do work." Well, *industry* is one thing in the spider which we should do well to imitate.

But *perseverance* is another thing in the spider that deserves our imitation. By perseverance we mean a determination not to be discouraged in anything we undertake. Some people will try to do a thing once or twice, and then, if they meet with difficulties, they give up at once and try no more. Now, no one will ever get to be either great or good in that way. We must expect difficulties and disappointments in everything we attempt to do; and if we fail the first time we must begin again, and so the second time, and the third time, and keep on beginning again until we do it. This is just what the spider does. If you sweep down its web to-day, it will begin right away again and spin another. And so it will go on, day after day, as often as its web may be swept down. The spider seems to understand, or at least to act upon, the idea contained in these simple lines,—

> "If at first you don't succeed,
>   Try, try again.
> Let your courage well appear;
> If you only persevere,
> You will conquer, never fear;
>   Try, try again.
>
> "Twice or thrice though you should fail,
>   Try again.
> If at last you would prevail,
>   Try again.
> When you strive, there's no disgrace
> Though you fail to win the race;
> Bravely, then, in such a case,
>   Try, try again.
>
> "Let the thing be e'er so hard,
>   Try again;
> Time will surely bring reward,
>   Try again.

> That which other folks can do,
> Why, with patience, may not you?
> Why, with patience, may not you?
> Try, try again."

This is just what the spider does. And if we only learn to do this well we shall be sure, with God's blessing, to succeed in every right thing we undertake. The old proverb says, "Perseverance conquers all things." And how many examples might be mentioned to show that this is true! When Robert Bruce was king of Scotland, the English armies were overrunning the land. Bruce tried hard to drive them out of his country, and to free his people from their yoke. But he was defeated in several battles. After one of these defeats, he sat down to mourn over his own misfortunes and those of his unhappy country. He began to despair of ever doing anything, and was concluding to give up the attempt and not try any more, when his eye lighted on a spider, in one corner of the room, trying to fasten a thread in a particular direction. As often as he fastened it it came loose, and as often as it came loose he fastened it again. The defeated warrior was very much interested in watching the spider's operations. He saw what wonderful perseverance this little creature had. It seemed as though nothing would discourage it. He counted, some say nineteen or twenty, and some say between sixty and seventy, times that the spider renewed its efforts to fasten the thread, till finally it succeeded. Then Bruce rose up and resolved to imitate the example of the spider, and to struggle for the liberty of his country till he succeeded or perished.

I remember reading once of a bird, of the bobolink species, that was confined with some canaries. When it heard the canaries sing, the bobolink tried to imitate them, but found it could not. Then it began a regular series of experiments, and, taking one note at a time, and trying till it mastered that, it went on till at last it actually learned all their notes, and could join in concert with the canaries, and sing just as well as they.

THE BLIND SCULPTOR.

We should think that it was quite impossible for a blind man ever to become a sculptor, and learn to carve out images of men and animals, from wood and stone, without ever being able to see them. But perseverance has accomplished even this, as it did in the case of the blind sculptor of Switzerland. This man was attacked with the small-pox when he was only five years old. It left him entirely blind. Before losing his sight, he had often played with those little figures which the Swiss people make, and had even tried to handle a knife and form some himself. When his sight was gone, he often thought about those images. Then he would take them in his hands, and feel them, and try to comfort himself for the loss of sight by measuring them with his fingers. He would feel them again and again, and turn them over in every way, till he was able, by degrees, to tell exactly, by the touch, the size and proportions of the figure. Then he began to think whether he could not succeed in supplying the loss of sight by the sense of touch. His father and mother were both dead; and, finding himself alone and destitute, he resolved, rather than beg, to try to support himself by his own exertions.

Taking a piece of wood and a chisel, he began to work. His first attempts were very troublesome and very trifling. Often would he destroy, by a single notch made too deep, a piece of work to which he had devoted long days of labour. Such difficulties would have discouraged most persons, but the blind man persevered. After many trials, he at length succeeded in using his chisel with a steady hand; and so carefully would he examine each fold of the drapery, one after another, and the shape of each limb, till he came, as it were, to *see*, by means of his fingers, the figure he was trying to copy.

Thus he went on by degrees, till he has reached what seems an almost incredible perfection; for he is able to engrave, from memory, the features of a face, and make one exactly like it. He is now seventy years old, but in good health, and works every day as in his youth. In his lifetime he has sculptured many hundred figures. He is happy, and contented with his lot, and his works remain as so many monuments of the wonderful triumph of perseverance over difficulties.

Its *industry* and *perseverance*, then, are the two good things in the spider which we shall do well to imitate. This was the first question we were to consider.

We come now to our *second question;* and that is this:—*What does the spider gain by its industry and perseverance?*

Solomon says, "The spider taketh hold with her hands, and is in kings' palaces." There are two things the spider gains by exercising these good qualities. It gains an *honourable place* and an *honest living*. A king's palace is an honourable place, and there the spider's industry brings her. I suppose there never was a king's palace built so grand and fine but what the spider took hold with her hands and found her way into it. All the soldiers and servants that might be set to guard and keep it could not prevent the spider from getting in. You know Solomon built a very magnificent palace for his queen, the daughter of Pharaoh, king of Egypt, and all the fine ladies of his court. And no doubt great pains were taken to keep out spiders and all such ugly insects. And when, after all his care and pains, Solomon looked up to the window of his palace, or to the corner of the beautiful pavilion that hung over his throne, and saw an old spider spreading out his web there, I dare say he felt very much vexed. But there he was, and there he would be. Or, if they swept him down and killed him, pretty soon there would be another in his place. So that, no doubt, the wise man spoke from his own experience when he said, "The spider taketh hold with her hands, and is in kings' palaces." The industry and perseverance of the spider gain her an honourable place.

And, at the same time, they gain for her an *honest living*. But now, I think, I see some serious, thoughtful child shaking his head, and saying softly to himself, "Well, I don't know exactly about that. It seems to me that this thing of setting traps for poor innocent flies, and catching and eating them, is not a very honest way of getting a living after all!" It would not be an honest way for us to get our living in such a way, but it *is* an honest way for the spider. Now, my dear children, the only correct rule by which to judge whether anything is right or wrong is to ask what the will of God is concerning it. God cannot will or order anything wrong; and whatever God does will, or order, you may be sure, is right. It would not be honest or right for you or me to get our living by robbing our fellow-creatures, because this is contrary to the will of God. His command to us is, "Thou shalt not steal." "Do violence to no man." But isn't it honest for the fisherman to throw his line or net into the river or sea, and get his living by catching the poor innocent fish? Certainly it is. God made the fish for this purpose. It is His will that they should be caught and eaten; and this makes it honest and right for the fisherman to get his living by catching them. Isn't it honest and right for the butcher to take the ox or the sheep to the slaughter-house and kill him? Certainly it is. God made them to be eaten. It is the will of God that they should be killed for our food; and this makes it honest and right for the butcher to get his living by killing them. And, just so, God made the flies for the spider to eat. It is the will of God that he should eat them. And, therefore, when he employs his industry and perseverance in spreading his web, and catching flies, he is gaining an honest living by it. An honourable place and an honest living are the two things which the spider gains by these qualities so worthy of our imitation.

But there is a *third question* we were to ask; and we are ready for it now. The third question is this:— *What may we gain by industry and perseverance in the use of the means in our power?* We may gain *a more honourable place, and a better life, than that of the spider, and we may gain these for others as well as ourselves.*

We may gain a more honourable place than the spider.

And what is this? It is a place in the great palace of the King of heaven. That is worth more than all the world—yes, more than ten thousand worlds—can give. It is spoken of, in the Bible, as a place which God has been preparing from the foundation of the world. Solomon's temple was very splendid, and yet it only took him seven years to build it. It is almost six thousand years since the world was made. And all this time God has been preparing that heavenly temple in which His people are to dwell for ever. How very glorious it must be! Oh, what an honour to gain a place there! All the most splendid palaces of earthly kings are only like toys and baby-houses in comparison with it. But you must not think, my dear children, because we speak of *gaining* a place there, that anything we can do—any works or goodness of ours—will secure this blessing for us. Oh, no. God gives it of His own free grace to poor sinners, such as we are, for the sake of what Jesus did and suffered for us. But we must repent of our sins, and believe in Jesus, and then be *industrious* and *persevering* in trying to learn and do His will, and we shall certainly gain this honourable place. In this way we may, like the spider, take hold with our hands, and be in the palace of the Great King. *That* will be indeed a more honourable place than ever the spider can gain. And how different our position will be there from that of the spider in an earthly palace! The spider is only in his place for a little while, but we shall be in God's palace for ever and ever. The spider, when he gets into a king's palace, has to keep out of sight in some dark corner, or immediately he is swept down, and turned out or killed. But if we enter God's palace, Jesus will take us everywhere about, and show us all the beautiful things there, and nobody will dare to hurt us, or send us away, or ask what business we have there. The spider's nature is not changed because he gets into a king's palace. He is none the better or prettier for being there. But it will be different with us if we gain a place in God's palace. Our nature will be changed before we enter there. Everything sinful will be taken away from us. Jesus, the King of that palace, will make us as good and as beautiful as He is Himself. He will make us *look* like Him, and He will make us *be* like Him. Can anything be thought of so delightful as this? Is it not truly a more honourable place than the spider's that we may gain for ourselves by *industry* and *perseverance* in serving God?

But then we may gain a *better life* too, as well as a more honourable place, than the spider gains in this way. No doubt the spider finds a good deal of enjoyment, such as it is, in its own mode of living. It would not suit us, indeed. We should find no pleasure in it. But God is so good, so full of love and happiness Himself, that every living thing He has made, even down to the very tiniest insect that moves, finds pleasure in the way of life appointed for it. With most of these, as with the spider, the enjoyment of life is of a very low kind. It is chiefly, if not entirely, enjoyment connected merely with eating and drinking. Now, it is true that this is a great deal better than no life or enjoyment at all. But, ah! how very different from this will the life and enjoyment be of those who "take hold with their hands" and gain a place in the palace of the King of kings. Their life will not be for a few days only, but for everlasting days. It will be *eternal life*. Nobody will know what this means till they come to find it out by experience. And their enjoyment will not be in eating and drinking, but in something far, far better. When St Paul was speaking about this once, he said, "The kingdom of God" (and by this he meant the happiness of heaven) "is not meat and drink, but righteousness, and peace, and joy in the Holy Ghost." The happiness of heaven will be found in knowing and loving God, in studying His wonderful works, in growing more and more like Him, and in serving Him according to His will. This is the kind of life the angels live. How noble, how glorious, how happy it must be! Oh, may we not well say that industry and perseverance in trying to serve God will gain for us a better life than they gain for the spider?

And then, by imitating the spider in this way, *we may help others to gain these blessings too*, as well as gain them ourselves. This is something the spider never can do. It lives for itself alone. The industry and perseverance with which it weaves its web, and catches flies, is *all* for itself, and *only* for itself. But it is different with us. And now we come to that part of the sermon which bears upon ourselves. Our missionary offering, we all feel, is one of the most interesting things connected with these happy anniversaries. In preparing these offerings we have room to exercise industry and perseverance. We make our offerings for the purpose of sending the Gospel to those who are living in "the dark places of the earth, which are full of the habitations of cruelty." And in sending the Gospel to these benighted people, like the spider, we are weaving a net; but of a very different kind from his, and for a very different purpose. He weaves his net to catch flies. We weave ours to catch immortal souls. He desires to catch flies that he may plunder them, and torture them, and put them to death. We desire to catch souls in the net of the Gospel to enrich them, and bless them, and make them happy for ever, in the palace of the King of heaven. Our object in doing this is beautifully expressed in one of our sweet anniversary hymns, which says,—

> " We bring our little offering;
> And, humble though it be,
> We ask our God to bless it
> On low and bended knee:
> Perhaps a Bible purchased
> With this, so freely given,
> May teach some wandering heathen child
> The way to God and heaven."

We *know* that this has been the result of our offering in one case, and we hope it may be so in many cases. You remember, my dear children, that the very first time we had a missionary offering at our anniversary, we sent part

ENCOURAGEMENT TO WORK.

of our collection to Africa, and part of it to China. Four or five years afterwards, just a few days before the time for holding another anniversary, we received a letter from one of our missionaries in China, giving a very interesting account of the conversion and happy death of a Chinese youth connected with the Mission school. This youth had been taken into the school to be supported and educated by means of the money sent out from our first missionary collection. After being there two or three years, he became a Christian. Then he was taken sick and died. But he died with a hope in Jesus. And it was very pleasant and encouraging to us to hear of such a result following from our first missionary offering. It seemed like a voice from heaven saying to us, "Go on in your good work; do not be discouraged; try all you can to send the Gospel to the poor souls perishing without it, and you shall reap a rich reward at last." Then let us "take hold with our hands" afresh in this blessed work. Let us imitate the industry and perseverance of the spider; and may God grant that we may both gain a place in the palace of the King of heaven for ourselves, and be the means of bringing a great many others there also, for Jesus' sake. Amen.

THE MARKS OF A BEN-ONI.

"She called his name Ben-oni; but his father called him Benjamin."—GEN. xxxv. 18.

THESE words were spoken of Rachel, Jacob's wife. Her youngest child had just been born: she was very sick, and was going to die. The little child was lying by her. She called to see it; she kissed it, and called his name Ben-oni. Ben-oni means, "the son of my sorrow." This child was about to occasion the death of his mother, and therefore she gave him this name. She was sorry to leave her husband, her family, and her friends; and this feeling of sorrow led her to call his name Ben-oni.

"But his father called him Benjamin." Benjamin means, "the son of a right hand." Our right hand is a great comfort and blessing to us. What could we do without a right hand?

Now, every child that is born into this world will be either a Ben-oni or a Benjamin. There is not much difference between these two names, but there is a great deal of difference between the natures which they represent. All these children here assembled are either Ben-onies, or Benjamins. These names refer to girls as well as to boys. You will all be children of sorrow or children of help and comfort to your parents.

Now, the great question for us to consider is, What are the marks of a Ben-oni or of a Benjamin?

We shall mention *four* things which may always be considered as the marks of a Ben-oni; and the opposite of these, of course, will be the marks of a Benjamin.

The *first* mark of a Ben-oni—" a child of sorrow "—is *ill-temper*.

Suppose you had to walk four or five miles with a pebble in your shoe; or suppose you had to wear a coat or dress with a pin sticking in it; or suppose you had to lie all night in bed with a porcupine by your side, sticking you with his sharp-pointed quills: what an uncomfortable thing it would be! But none of these things are so uncomfortable as to be connected with an ill-temper. An ill-temper is the most uncomfortable thing in the world. We can protect ourselves against many uncomfortable things. Thus we put roofs on our houses to keep the rain off, which would be uncomfortable; we put doors and windows in our houses to keep the cold and wind out, which would be uncomfortable; but how are we to keep bad tempers out of our houses? All peevish, cross, ill-natured children are Ben-onies—children of sorrow to their parents and the families where they dwell.

There were two little boys in a Southern city, whose names were Augustus and Eugene. They were playing top, and had but one between them, which they spun alternately. At first they played very pleasantly, but soon became very angry, and began to speak unkindly. Eugene said, " It's my turn to spin the top now."

" No, it's not; it's mine !" said Augustus.

Then they grew very angry about it. Augustus then said to Eugene,—

" You lie !"

Then Eugene struck him, and Augustus struck him back again. They seized each other in great rage, and, in the scuffle, Eugene took a long sharp knife from his pocket and stabbed Augustus, so that he died in a few moments. Augustus lost his life, and Eugene became a murderer, merely to decide whose turn it was to spin a top. There was ill-temper; and what a Ben-oni that ill-temper made him to his parents and to the family to which he belonged!

There was a rich nobleman in England who had a little daughter named Anne. They were very fond of her; for she was a fine little creature, very lively, and merry, and affectionate, and exceedingly beautiful. But she had a very ill temper. When anything vexed her she would fly into a rage, and turn and strike any one that provoked her. After every fit of anger she would be ashamed and sorry, and resolve never to do so again. But the next time she was provoked it was all forgotten, and she was as angry as ever. When she was between four and five years of age, her mother had a little son, a sweet little tender baby. Anne's nurse, who was thoughtless and wicked, loved to tease her, because she was so easily irritated; and so she told her that her father and mother would not care for her now, because all their love and pleasure would be in this little brother, and they would not mind her. Poor Anne burst into a flood of tears, and cried bitterly, saying, "You are a naughty woman to say so! Mamma will always love me; I know she will, and I'll go this very moment and ask her." And she ran out of the nursery and hastened to her mother's room. The servant called after her: "Come, miss, you needn't go to your mother's room; she won't see you now." Anne burst open the door, but was instantly caught hold of by a strange woman she had never seen before. "My dear," said this woman, "you cannot see your mother just now;" and she was going on to tell that it was because she was very sick, and could not be disturbed. But she was too angry to listen; and she screamed and kicked at the woman, who was obliged to take her by force and carry her back to the nursery. When she put her down she gave the servant a charge not to let her go to her mother's room. This added to her rage. But the thoughtless, wicked servant, instead of trying to soothe and quiet her, burst out into a laugh, and said, "I told you that, miss. You see your mamma does not love you now." Then the poor child became mad with fury. She seized a smoothing-iron, and, darting forward, threw it upon the baby's head as it lay in the cradle. The child gave one struggle, and breathed no more.

Anne's mother died that night of grief. Anne grew up in the possession of great riches. She had every outward comfort about her that money could procure; but she was a very unhappy and miserable woman. She was never known to smile. The thought of the terrible consequences of that one outburst of passion pressed upon her like a heavy burden all her days. Ah! what a Benoni this girl became! She was a child of sorrow to her parents. Her ill-temper made her so. If you give way to such tempers, my dear young friends, you will certainly be Ben-onies; but if you strive and pray against such feelings, and try to be gentle, kind, and pleasant to those around you, then you will be Benjamins,—children of the right hand to your parents. See, now, how differently such children will act.

A gentleman was walking on the Battery, in the city of New York, one day, and, as he passed a little girl who was cheerfully rolling her hoop, he said to her, "You are a nice little girl;" to which she replied, patting her little brother on the head, "And Bobbie is a nice little brother, too." Here was good-temper, which would make this dear child "a child of the right hand" to her parents, and cause her to be loved by all who were about her.

A mother, who was in the habit of asking her children, before they retired at night, what they had done to make others happy, found her young twin-daughters silent.

She spoke tenderly of habits and dispositions founded on the Golden Rule, "Do unto others as you would have them do to you." Still these bright little faces were bowed in silence. The question was repeated. "I cannot remember anything good all this day, dear mother," said one of the little girls; "only one of my class-mates was happy because she had gained the head of the class, and I smiled on her, and ran to kiss her. She said I was good; that is all, dear mother."

The other spoke still more tenderly:—"A little girl, who sat with me on the bench at school, lost a little brother; and I saw that, while she studied her lesson, she hid her face in the book and wept. I felt sorry, and laid my face on the same book, and wept with her. Then she looked up, and was comforted, and put her arms around my neck; but I do not know why she said I had done her good."

These were children of good tempers,—children whose pleasant dispositions would make them children of the right hand to their parents,—real Benjamins indeed.

Ill-temper, then, is the first mark of a Ben-oni—a child of sorrow.

The *second* mark of a Ben-oni is *idleness*.

Idle children love to lie in bed in the morning; they love to do nothing all day, if they can help it, but play.

It is a great trouble to get them to study, to read, or to work. Now, idle children always make idle men; for the habits which children form while they are children will surely remain with them when they grow up to be men and women.

John Alsop was about fifteen years old when his father, who had just moved into a new settlement, was clearing land. One day the father and a neighbour were engaged in building a log-fence, which was made of the trunks of the trees that were cleared off the lands. First they laid the fence one log high, with the ends of each length passing a little way by each other. Notches were cut in the ends, and a block was laid crosswise, where the ends lapped, and then another tier was laid on the cross-pieces, till the fence was high enough. To roll up the top logs, they would lay long poles, called *skids*, one end on the top of the logs and the other on the ground, and roll up the logs on these. But as the logs were very heavy, they were obliged to stop several times to rest, or to get a new hold; and it was John's business, when they stopped, to put a block under the log, to keep it from rolling back. Having given a hard lift, and tugging with all his might, the father called out, "There, Johnny! put under your block!—quick!" Johnny started nimbly, and snatched up his block, when, suddenly, the chirp of a little squirrel struck his ear. Instantly down went his block, and away he ran after the squirrel, leaving his father and the other man to hold the log till he came back. This anecdote gives you John's character. He was an idle boy. He had no fondness for work; he was not willing to follow any one object or pursuit long enough to accomplish anything. Thirty years after this, a gentleman who had known him in his youthful days inquired about him of one of his neighbours, who related this anecdote, and added, "*He has been running after squirrels ever since.*" He never was steady and persevering in the pursuit of anything. When he was a young man he never could make up his mind decidedly what employment to follow. He had no industry; he would try one thing a little while, get tired of it, and then take up another; but followed no business long enough to get well acquainted with it. He has always been *hunting the squirrel.*

Now, we are to remember, dear children, that God is busy at all times, and almost everything that God has made is busy. Look at the sun; it is always at work, shining and shining and shining from one year's end to the other. In the daytime it is shining in our part of the world, and when it is night to us it is shining in the opposite part of the world. And so it is with the moon, —always shining in one part of the world or the other. So it is with the sea; its waves are rising, and falling, and rolling, and flowing continually. So it is with the rivers; they are continually running, from the fountains where they spring, on, on to the ocean. And so it is with the little birds, and little fishes, and the bees, and the ants: none of these are idle.

Idleness always leads to ignorance, and poverty, and uselessness, dear children, and idle persons never do anything good to themselves or to others. They never succeed in business; they never get on in life.

A gentleman in England had an estate which was worth over two hundred pounds a-year. For a while he kept his farm in his own hands, but at length found himself so much in debt that he was obliged to sell one-half of his place to pay up. The rest he let out to a farmer for several years. Towards the end of that time, the farmer, on coming to pay his rent, asked him whether he would sell his farm. The gentleman was surprised that the farmer should be able to make him an offer for his place. "Pray, tell me," said he, "how it happens that, while I could not live upon twice as much land, for which I paid no rent, you are regularly paying me about one hundred pounds a-year for the farm, and able in a few years to purchase it?" "The reason is plain," answered the farmer; "it lies in the difference between '*go*' and '*come.*'" "I do not understand you," said the gentleman. "I mean," said the farmer, "that you sat still and said, *Go;* I get up and say, *Come.* You lie in bed, and enjoy your ease; I rise early in the morning, and attend to my business." In other words, this was an industrious man; there was no love of idleness about him, and this led to his success in life.

I remember another anecdote, which plainly shows the advantages of industry.

There was once a young man who was commencing life as a clerk. One day his employer said to him, "Now, to-morrow that cargo of cotton must be got out and weighed, and we must have a regular account of it." He was an industrious young man,—a young man of great energy. This was the first time he had been intrusted with the superintendence of work like this. He made his arrangements the night before, spoke to the men about their carts and horses, and resolved to begin very early the next day. He instructed the labourers to be there at half-past four o'clock in the morning. They set to work, and the thing was done; and about ten or eleven o'clock the master came in, and saw the young man sitting in the counting-house, and looked very black at him, supposing his commands had not been executed. "I thought," said he, "you were instructed to get out that cargo this morning?" "It is all done, sir," said the young man, "and here is the account of it." This one act made that young man's fortune. It fixed his character. It gave his employer a confidence in him that was never shaken. He found him to be a man of industry, a man of promptness, and he very soon found that he was one that could not be spared; he was necessary to the concerns of that establishment, and became one of the partners. He was a religious man, and went through a life of great benevolence, and at his deathbed was able to leave his children an ample fortune. His industry made him a Benjamin indeed.

And just as idle boys will grow up to be idle men, so will idle girls grow up to be idle women. They will be of no use to themselves, and of no use to anybody else. But those who form early habits of industry will certainly rise to honour, usefulness, and happiness.

Miss Rachel Cowe was the daughter of a wealthy man, engaged in an extensive business. He lived in Aberdeen, Scotland. But, in that country, the females of many families in the higher ranks of life, as well as those in middling circumstances, were instructed in some branch of business suited to their strength and capacity—an excellent custom; for, whatever may be our circumstances to-day, we know not what they may be to-morrow; riches are no sure dependence, for they often "take to themselves wings and fly away."

Rachel Cowe was early put to learn a branch of the millinery business. This she industriously acquired, though she knew not that she should ever need it. But, after a while, her father's business began to decline, and at length he failed. He gave up to his creditors everything but their wearing-apparel and a few books. Both her parents were left with no means of support in their old age. There was no one now but herself on whom they could depend. When Rachel saw the decline of her father's business, she obtained his consent to set up her own. She had a small sum of money, and she borrowed a little more from a friend, to begin with. She began her business, praying that God would prosper it, and keep her from the new temptations to which she would be exposed. She was successful. In a few months she was able to pay what she had borrowed and to furnish a house for herself. When her father's business completely failed, and her parents were thrown upon the world, destitute of the means of support, she was prepared to receive them into her own house. She supported them by her labours, she nursed them with the utmost tenderness in their illness, she attended them in their last sickness, and saw them die in the hope of glory. What a child of comfort was this industrious girl to her parents! And this is not all. While they lived, she would listen to no proposals of marriage; but, after their death, she became the wife of the Rev. Dr Milne, and accompanied him on his mission to China, where she was a great solace and comfort to him, and a helper to him in his labours. Thus the industrious girl became the industrious woman; and I would have you all, my dear girls, to follow her example.

Yes; idleness is the second mark of a Ben-oni.

The *third* mark of a Ben-oni is *pride*.

Some children are proud of their clothes. This is very silly indeed; for the butterflies have much more beautiful clothes than we, and yet they are never proud of their dress. Some children are proud of their families. This also is very silly, for we have all sprung at first from one father. Some children are proud about their houses. This, too, is very silly, for, by-and-by, they will all crumble into the dust, from which they have been taken, while the grave is the one house to which we must all come at last.

Proud children feel and think themselves better than

others, and are often unwilling to engage in honest and honourable employments.

Listen to what I am going to tell you.

Chief-Justice Marshall was a great man; but great men are never proud. He was not too proud to wait upon himself. He was in the habit of going to market himself, and carrying home his purchases. Often he would be seen returning at sunrise with poultry in one hand and vegetables in the other. On one of these occasions a fashionable young man from the North, who had removed to Richmond, was swearing violently because he could find no one to carry home his turkey. Judge Marshall stepped up and asked him where he lived. When he heard, he said, "That is in my way, and I will take your turkey home for you." When they came to the house the young man inquired, "What shall I pay you?" "Oh, nothing," said the Judge; "you are welcome; it was all in the way, and it was no trouble to me." "Who is that polite old gentleman who brought home my turkey for me?" asked the young man of a by-stander. "Oh," said he, "that was Judge Marshall, Chief-Justice of the United States." "Why did *he* bring home my turkey?" "He did it," said the by-stander, "to give you a rebuke, and teach you to attend to your own business."

True greatness never feels above doing anything that is useful; but especially the truly great man will never feel above helping himself; his own independence of character depends upon his being able to help himself. The great Dr Franklin, when he first established himself in business in Philadelphia, wheeled home the paper which he purchased for his printing-office upon a wheelbarrow with his own hands.

Pride, then, bear in mind, children, is the *third* mark of a Ben-oni.

The *fourth* and only other mark that we shall speak of is *disobedience*.

There is nothing on which the comfort and happiness

of parents and families depend more than on the *obedience* of children.

My dear children, if you want to plant thorns on the pillows of your parents, and plunge daggers into their bosoms, be disobedient. If you want to make them as uncomfortable as they possibly can be in this world, then be disobedient. This is the *chief* mark of a Ben-oni.

I remember reading not long ago of a gentleman in England who had two sons. He was a kind, excellent, pious man, and did everything for the comfort of his children that he thought it right to do. But sometimes the boys were anxious to do things which their parents were not willing that they should do. One Sunday, the eldest boy went to his father and asked permission to take the carriage and go riding in the afternoon, instead of going to church.

His father told him he could not, because it would be breaking the Sabbath. The boy was very much displeased because his father would not let him go riding, as some of the boys in the neighbourhood had been allowed by their parents to do. He was so wicked about this that he determined no longer to stay at home, because his father would not let him do just what he wanted. So the next day he persuaded his brother to go with him, and they went down to Portsmouth, a town by the seaside, intending to go to sea.

Before going, however, they called on the Rev. Mr Griffin, to assist them to get a situation on board a man-of-war. This good man, perceiving that they were not accustomed to the mode of life in which they were about to enter, inquired of them their object in going to sea. The eldest boy frankly told him they were going *in order to spite their parents !* Then he told him the story of what had taken place at home—of his father's unwillingness to allow him to ride on Sunday—and said he was going to sea in order to make his father feel sorry for refusing to gratify him. The good clergyman tried to show them the

DISOBEDIENCE TO PARENTS.

guilt and folly of the course they were about to pursue, and to set before them the unavoidable consequences that would result from it. The younger son was impressed by the counsels and advice of the clergyman, and went home; but the elder son resolved to go on in his evil course.

Some twelve or fifteen years after this had taken place, this same clergyman was called to the prison in the town of Portsmouth to see a sailor who was condemned to be executed, and who was going to be hung in a few days.

When he entered the cell of the prison he saw a wretched, miserable, squalid-looking creature sitting by a table in the cell, who looked up to him as he entered, and said, "Do you not remember me, sir?" "No," said the clergyman; "I do not recollect that I ever saw you before." Then the poor man recalled to him the story of the boy who went from home in order to spite his parents. "And are you the miserable man," said the clergyman, "who did this?" "Yes," said the poor culprit; "I followed out my own plan; I went on the course which I had chosen, contrary to your advice and to my own convictions; I plunged into all sorts of wickedness and sin, and finally became involved in a robbery and murder, for which I am now about to suffer the penalty. And all this in consequence of my disobedience to my parents!" The clergyman wrote to the father of this unhappy man, who came to visit his son in his last hours, and who had the unspeakable anguish of standing by and seeing him suffer the penalty of the law, and reap the bitter fruits of his disobedience.

What a Ben-oni that son was to his father!

I have another story to tell you of a disobedient son, in order to illustrate the point on which we are now speaking.

The youth of whom I am about to speak was the son of a sea-captain. His father had been absent from home on a long voyage. During his absence his child had grown from being an infant into a rough and careless boy. He was becoming restive under his mother's control; her gentle voice no longer restrained him. He was often wilful, and sometimes disobedient. He thought it showed a manly superiority to be independent of a mother's influence.

About this time his father came home; and it was very fortunate that he did return. He soon perceived the spirit of disobedience that was stirring in his son. The boy saw that it displeased his father, although, for a few days, he said nothing about it.

One afternoon in October, a bright, golden day, the father told his son to get his hat and take a walk with him. They turned down an open field, a favourite playground for the children in the neighbourhood. After talking cheerfully on different topics for a while (said the boy, who gives this history of himself), my father asked me if I observed that great shadow thrown by a huge mass of rock that stood in the middle of the field. I replied that I did. "*My* father owned that land," said he; "it was my playground when a boy. The rock stood there then; to me it is a beacon, and whenever I look at it I recall a dark spot in my life,—an event so painful to dwell upon, that, were it not as a warning to you, I should not speak of it. Listen, then, my dear boy, and learn wisdom from your father's experience.

"My father died when I was a mere child. I was the only son. My mother was a gentle, loving woman, devoted to her children, and beloved by everybody.

"I remember her pale, beautiful face, her sweet, affectionate smile, her kind and gentle voice. In my childhood I loved her sincerely. I was never happy apart from her; and she, fearing that I was becoming too much of a child, sent me to a high-school in the village.

"After associating for a time with rude, rough boys, I lost, in a measure, my fondness for home and my reverence for my mother; and it became more and more difficult for her to restrain my impetuous nature. I thought it indicated a want of manliness to yield to her control or to appear penitent, although I knew that my conduct pained her.

"The epithet I most feared was *girl-boy*. I could not bear to hear it said by my playmates that I was 'tied to my mother's apron-strings.'

"From a quiet, home-loving child I became a wild, boisterous boy.

"My mother was very anxious to induce me to seek happiness within the precincts of home. She exerted herself to make our fireside attractive; and my sister, following her self-sacrificing example, sought to entice me by planning games and diversions for my amusement and entertainment. I saw all this, but did not heed it until it was too late.

"It was on an afternoon like this, as I was about leaving the dining-table to spend the intermission between morning and evening school in the street, as usual, my mother laid her hand on my shoulder and said, mildly, but firmly, 'My son, I wish you to come with me.'

"I would have rebelled, but something in her manner awed me.

"She put on her bonnet, and said to me, 'We will take a little walk together.' I followed her in silence, and, as I was passing out of the door, I observed one of my rude companions skulking about the house, and I knew he was waiting for me. He sneered as I passed by him. My pride was wounded to the quick. He was a very bad boy, and, being some years older than myself, he exercised a great influence over me.

"I followed my mother sulkily till we reached the spot where we now stand, beneath the shadow of this huge rock.

"Oh, my boy, could that hour be blotted from my memory, which has cast a dark shadow over my whole life, gladly would I exchange all that the world can offer me for the quiet peace of mind I should enjoy! But no! Like this huge, unsightly pile stands the monument of my guilt for ever.

"My mother, being in feeble health, sat down, and beckoned me to sit down beside her. Her look, so full of tender sorrow, is present to me now.

"I would not sit, but still continued standing beside her.

"'Alfred, my dear son,' she said, 'have you lost all your love for your mother?'

"I did not reply.

"'I fear you have,' she continued; 'and may God help you to see your own heart, and me to do my duty!'

"She then talked to me of my misdeeds,—of the dreadful consequences of the course I was pursuing. By tears and entreaties and prayers she tried to make an impression upon me. She placed before me the lives and examples of great and good men. She sought to stimulate my ambition.

"I was moved, but too proud to show it, and remained standing in dogged silence beside her. I thought, What will my companions say if, after all my boasting, I should yield at last, and submit to be led by a woman?

"What agony was in my mother's face when she saw that all she had said and suffered failed to move me!

"She rose to go home, and I followed at a distance. She spoke no more to me until we reached our own door.

"'It is school-time now,' she said; 'go, my son, and once more let me beseech you to think upon what I have said.'

"'I sha'n't go to school,' said I.

"She looked astonished at my boldness, but replied, firmly,—

"'Certainly you will go, Alfred; I command you.'

"'I will not,' said I, with a tone of defiance.

"'One of two things you must do, Alfred. Either go to school this moment, or I will lock you up in your room, and keep you there until you are ready to promise obedience to my wishes.'

"'I dare you to do it,' said I; 'you can't get me upstairs.'

"'Alfred, choose now,' said my mother, who laid her hand on my arm. She trembled violently, and was deadly pale.

"'If you touch me I will kick you!' said I, in a terrible rage.

"'Will you go, Alfred?'

"'No,' replied I, but quailed beneath her glance.

"'Then follow me,' said she, as she grasped my arm firmly.

"I raised my foot—oh, my boy, hear me!—I raised my foot and kicked her—my sainted mother!

"Oh, my head reels as the torrent of memory rushes over me! I kicked my mother,—a feeble woman,—*my mother!*

"She staggered back a few steps, and leaned against the wall. She did not look at me. I saw her heart beat against her breast.

"'Oh, heavenly Father,' she cried, 'forgive him! he knows not what he does!'

"The gardener just then passing the door, and seeing my mother pale and almost unable to support herself, he stopped. She beckoned him in.

"'Take this boy up-stairs, and lock him in his own room,' she said, and turned from me.

"Looking back as she was entering her own room, she gave me such a look!—it will for ever follow me. It was a look of agony, mingled with the deepest love. It was the last unutterable pang from a heart that was broken.

"In a moment I found myself a prisoner in my own room. I thought for a moment I would fling myself out of the window and dash my brains out; but I felt afraid to die. I was not penitent. At times my heart was subdued, but my stubborn pride rose in an instant and bade me not to yield. The pale face of my mother haunted me. I flung myself on my bed and fell asleep. I awoke at midnight, suffering with the damp night air and terrified with frightful dreams. I would have sought my mother at that moment, for I trembled with fear; but my door was fast.

"With the daylight my terrors were dissipated, and I became bold in resisting all good impulses. The servant brought my meals, but I did not taste them. I thought the day would never end.

"Just at twilight I heard a light footstep approach the door. It was my sister, who called me by name.

"'What may I tell mother for you?' she asked.

"'Nothing,' I replied.

"'Oh, Alfred, for my sake, and for all our sakes, say that you are sorry; she longs to forgive you.'

"'I won't be driven to school against my will,' I replied.

"'But you will go if mother wishes it, dear Alfred?' my sister said, pleadingly.

"'No, I won't,' said I; 'and you needn't say another word about it.'

"'Oh, brother, you will kill her! you will kill her! and then you can never have a happy moment!'

"I made no reply to this. My feelings were touched, but I still resisted their influence. My sister called me, but I would not answer. I heard her footsteps slowly retreating, and again I flung myself upon my bed and passed another wretched and fearful night. Oh, God, how wretched—how fearful—I did not know!

"Another footstep, slower and feebler than my sister's, disturbed me. A voice called my name. It was my mother's.

"'Alfred, my son, shall I come in? Are you sorry for what you have done?' she asked.

"I cannot tell what influence, operating at that time, made me speak adverse to my feelings.

"The gentle voice of my mother that thrilled through me melted the ice from my obdurate heart, and I longed to throw myself upon her neck; but I did not. No, my boy, I did not! But my words gave the lie to my heart when I said I was not sorry.

"I heard her withdraw. I heard her groan. I longed to call her back, but I did not.

"I was awakened from an uneasy slumber by hearing my name called loudly, and my sister stood by my bedside.

"'Get up, Alfred; oh, do not wait a moment! Get up and come with me; mother is dying!'

"I thought I was dreaming, but I got up mechanically, and followed my sister.

"On the bed, pale and cold as marble, lay my mother. She had not undressed. She had thrown herself on the bed to rest. Rising to go again to me, she was seized with a palpitation of the heart, and borne senseless to her room.

"I cannot tell you my agony as I looked upon her. My remorse was tenfold more bitter from the thought that she would never know it. I believed myself to be a murderer. I fell on the bed beside her. I could not weep. My heart burned in my bosom; my brain was all on fire. My sister threw her arms around me and wept in silence. Suddenly we saw a slight motion of mother's hand. Her eyes unclosed. She had recovered consciousness, but not speech. She looked at me, and moved her lips; I could not understand her words.

"'My mother,' I shrieked, 'say only that you forgive me!'

"She could not say it with her lips, but her hands pressed mine. She smiled upon me; and, lifting her thin white hands, clasped my own within them, and cast her eyes upward. She moved her lips in prayer, and thus she died.

"I remained still kneeling before that dear form till my gentle sister removed me. She comforted me, for she knew the heavy load of sorrow at my heart—heavier than grief at the loss of a mother, for it was a load of sorrow for sin.

"The joy of youth had left me for ever."

My father ceased speaking, and buried his face in his hands. He saw and felt the bearing of his narrative upon my character and conduct.

I have never forgotten it; and I would say to boys who spurn a mother's control, who are ashamed to own that they are wrong, who think it manly to resist her authority or to oppose her influence: "Beware! Lay not up for yourselves bitter memories for your future years."

That was a Ben-oni indeed,—a child of sorrow to his parent, to his sister, and to all around him. His disobedience made him such.

Let us look, now, at one or two examples of an opposite character.

William Hale was an obedient son. He was spending some time with his mother at the Saratoga Springs, and had become acquainted with a number of boys of his own age there.

One day some half-dozen of the children were playing on the piazza, and one of them was heard exclaiming,—

"Oh, yes, that's capital! So we will; come on, now! Where's William Hale? Come on, Will! We are going to have a ride on the circular railroad. Come with us."

"Yes, if my mother is willing," said William. "I will run and ask her."

"Ah, ah! so you must run and ask your *ma!*—great baby-boy!—run along to your ma! Ain't you ashamed?"

"I don't ask my mother," said one.

"Neither do I," said another.

"Neither do I," said a third.

"Be a man, Will, and come along," said the first boy, "if you don't wish to be called a coward as long as you live; don't you see we are all waiting?"

William was standing with one foot advanced, and his hand firmly clenched, in the midst of the group. His brow was flushed, his eye was flashing, his lip was compressed, his cheek was changing—all showing how the epithet "coward" rankled in his bosom.

It was doubtful for a moment whether he would have the true bravery to be called a coward rather than to do

AN EXAMPLE OF TRUE COURAGE.

wrong; but, with a voice trembling with emotion, he replied,—

"I will not go without I ask my mother; and I am no coward, either. I promised her I would not go from the house without her permission; and I should be a base coward if I were to tell my mother a lie."

When William returned to his mother to ask her permission to go, and told her of what had taken place, she threw her arms around his neck, and exclaimed,—

"God bless you, my dear child, and give you grace always to act in this way."

Ah, my dear children, he was a Benjamin—a child of comfort—to his dear mother; and doubtless he grew up to be her support and comfort all her days.

After the surrender of Cornwallis, and the victory achieved by the American arms, George Washington, when the war was over, returned in triumph to his mother's home. Everybody was honouring him and praising him as the saviour of his country and the greatest man of the age. When he reached the place of his mother's abode a large concourse of the people had met to greet him and welcome him to his home. In the centre of the assembled crowd stood his mother, and, pushing his way through the crowd around him, he hastened to pay her his respects; and, as she threw her arms around his neck and kissed him, she said to some who were congratulating her upon having so noble a son,—

"George always was an obedient child."

He was indeed a Benjamin—a son of comfort—to his mother, and a blessing to the country and to the world; and the spirit of obedience early learned and early practised was that which went to make him what he was.

And now, in conclusion, my dear children, let me ask you, Which of these two do you desire to be? Will you be Ben-onies—children of sorrow and grief—to your parents? or will you be Benjamins—children of joy and comfort and blessing—to them? If you would be the latter,—Benjamins indeed,—then you must watch and strive and pray against all the evils of which we have been speaking. Watch against these four marks of a Ben-oni:—watch against *ill-temper*, watch against *idleness*, watch against *pride*, watch against *disobedience;* and pray God to enable you each to overcome all these evils,—to erase these marks of a Ben-oni as they are beginning to fasten themselves on your character, and to earn for yourself the character of a Benjamin indeed.

THE CROOKED THINGS STRAIGHTENED.

" That which is crooked cannot be made straight."—
ECCLESIASTES, i. 15.

THIS does not mean that no crooked thing can ever be straightened, for we all know very well that this is not true. It is easy enough to straighten *some* crooked things. Here, for instance, is a piece of paper. I can take it in my hand, and squeeze and crumple it all up till there is not one straight piece in it as big as your little-finger nail. And then I can spread it out on the table, and smooth it down, and make it just as straight again as ever it was. Or here is a piece of dough, or a bit of clay. I can roll it out and twist it round till it is as crooked as a ram's horn. Now, if I put it into the oven, and bake it while it is in this state, why, then our text will apply to it, and "that which is crooked cannot be made straight." But before it gets thus hardened, I can take and roll it out between the palms of my hands, and make it as smooth and straight as I want it to be. And just so, if I take a tender willow twig, I can wind it round my finger like a thread; then I can unwind it again, and it will come out as straight as ever. But let that willow twig remain crooked while it is growing for five or ten years, and then you may write on it the words of our text; for "that which is crooked cannot be made straight." Now, God compares Himself in the Bible to a potter and His people to clay. God compares Himself to a gardener and His people to plants or trees which He has planted. And as it is true of clay and of trees that if you begin at the right time and take proper pains you can straighten what is crooked in them, so it is true of boys and girls. And as it is true of clay and trees that if you let the one get baked or the other grow old while it is crooked you cannot straighten it, just so it is true of boys and girls. How very important, then, it is for us to know what there is crooked about ourselves, and how we may get it straightened! I have chosen this text on purpose to help us to understand this matter. And there are *four* things which I wish especially to show you while talking about these words of Solomon.

The first thing I wish to show is that we are all born with crooked hearts.

What sort of hearts are we born with? Crooked hearts. But some of you may be ready to ask, Well, what sort of a heart is a crooked heart? Why, a crooked heart is a wicked or sinful heart. I say, then, we are all born with sinful or wicked hearts. Now, a great many people don't believe this; but it is just as true as that two and two make four. I can prove this to you, my dear children, in two ways. I can prove it *from the Bible*, and then I can prove it *without the Bible*.

Now, I might point you to a good many places in the Bible which prove that we are born with sinful hearts; but I will only point you to two. In the fifty-first Psalm, and fifth verse, David tells us that he was born a sinner. But David was born just as you and I and all of us were. His heart or nature was just the same at his birth as ours is. And if some of you think that perhaps David was born with a heart more crooked or sinful than other people, and that perhaps some children are born with a heart that is not at all sinful, I can show you from another passage of Scripture that this is not the case. The apostle Paul tells us in Ephesians, second chapter, and third verse, that " we are *all by nature* the children of wrath." Now, when he tells us here what we are "*by nature*," he means what we are at the time we are born. And when he says

THE CROOKED TREES.—*Rills from the Fountain of Life*, p. 52.

BIBLE PROOFS OF CROOKED HEARTS. 53

we are "the children of wrath," he means that we are born children with whom God is angry. But God is never angry with people for anything but for sin. And if God is angry with us when we are born, then it is very certain that we must be born sinners. This is enough, then, to prove from the Bible that we are all born with crooked, sinful hearts.

But, then, I said we can prove this *without the Bible;* and so we can. Now, there are two things about children which show that they are born with crooked, sinful hearts, even if the Bible had never said anything about it. *The sufferings and death of children* prove it; and *the way in which children grow up* proves it.

See, here is a cradle with a dear little infant in it, fast asleep. Look at its little dimpled chin, its rosy, rounded cheeks, its ruby lips, and golden locks. How sweet, how beautiful, how like a little cherub it seems! As we stand and gaze upon it, admiring its loveliness and feeling tempted to stoop down and kiss the little darling, we are tempted to ask ourselves, Can there be anything crooked or sinful in this sweet sleeping child? But see; while we are looking at it a change passes over the smiling face of the baby. An expression of pain appears upon it. It starts up with a sharp, piercing cry. It rolls about in agony. Its screams fill the house. Convulsions have taken it. Nothing that its anxious mother can do affords it any relief. It struggles for a few short hours with the painful disease, and then it dies. But suffering and death never come where there is no sin. Do the angels in heaven ever get sick? Oh, no. Did an angel ever die? No. Are there any graveyards in heaven? None at all. But why not? Why is there no sickness, or suffering, or death among the angels? Because there is nothing crooked, nothing sinful, about them. And why do infants sicken and suffer and die? Because they are born with crooked, sinful hearts. Yes, my dear children, every time you hear an infant cry you hear an argument which proves that we are all born sinners. Every time you see an infant's coffin, an infant's funeral, or an infant's grave, you see a certain proof that we are all born sinners. The sufferings and death of children prove it without the Bible.

And then the way in which children grow up proves it also. All children grow up to be bad if they are left to themselves. Since the world began there never was a child born and left to grow up as it pleased that grew up to love and serve God. Now, this proves something or other, and it is very easy to tell what it proves. If you go into a garden and see the sweet-smelling mignonette growing around one of the beds, what kind of seed, do you know, must have been sowed there? Mignonette seed. If you pluck a sweet, juicy apple from a tree, what sort of a tree must it be from which you plucked it? A sweet apple-tree. If you pluck an apple from another tree, and find it to be a sour crab-apple, what kind of a tree must that be on which it grew? A crab-apple-tree. How do you know this? By its fruit. Do apples or peaches ever grow on thorn-bushes? No. If the berries that grow upon a certain bush, or the fruit on a certain tree, are always poisonous, what sort of a bush or tree must that be? Poisonous. Now, our actions may be compared to fruit, and our hearts to the trees on which they grow. And if we find that, in all countries and in all ages, children left to themselves grow up only to bear evil fruit,—the fruit of opposition to God's law and hatred to God's character,—what must their hearts be which bring forth these wicked fruits? They must be wicked hearts. For as the tree is known by its fruit, so is the heart known by the actions which it leads men to perform. And in this way we can prove, both from the Bible and without the Bible, that we are all born with crooked or sinful hearts.

This is the first of the four things I wish to show you while talking about our text.

And now we come to the *second* of these things. It is this: *that, like the tree or the clay, our hearts are having something done to them which will make it much harder to straighten what is crooked in them.* With the tree, it is its growth that will make its crookedness hard to straighten. With the clay, it is the baking or burning of it. With ourselves, it is the exercising or practising of what is sinful in our hearts that will make it hard to straighten them. There is a kind of education for our hearts to go through. When we are acquiring learning of any kind we call it getting an education. And the places where we learn things we call schools. And there are a great many different kinds of schools. There are the common schools, where we learn the things necessary to make us useful in life. And there are medical schools, where young men go to learn to become doctors; and law schools, where they learn to become lawyers; and divinity schools, where they learn to become ministers. And then the shops in which the mechanics learn their trades are a kind of school. The carpenter's shop is a school to him; and so is the blacksmith's shop and the tailor's shop a school. Wherever we learn to think, or say, or do anything, that is a school to us. Now, a great many children never go to school anywhere but on the playground and at the corners of the streets. There they learn to do wicked things. All that is crooked in their hearts becomes fixed in their crookedness. There the crooked parts of their nature get educated. There the little twigs of evil in them grow into great, strong limbs that nobody can bend. There the clay of their nature gets baked and hardened before it is straightened. The habits we form and the characters we acquire while we are young will remain with us when we grow up to be men and women. And so the habits and characters we form in this world will remain with us after death in the world which we must enter then. This world is God's school. All the time spent in it is time spent at school. We are getting educated here for eternity. And when we form a wrong habit of thinking, or feeling, or acting, we are hardening a crooked point and fastening it upon our characters. And when we go out of the school of life,—that is, when we come to die and go into eternity,—then it will be true that "that which is crooked cannot be made straight." If the potter is making a pitcher, and finds that the handle or side of it has got out of shape and crooked, he can very easily alter it and make it straight again if he only finds it out *before* it has been put into the oven and baked. But if he does not see it till *after* it comes out of the oven, then there is no help for it. However strangely out of shape it may be, it must remain so. Then he knows that "that which is crooked cannot be made straight." And so it is with the gardener and his trees. While they are young and tender it is very easy to straighten them when they get crooked. But let them only *grow* crooked, and then what can he do with them? One of the crookedest trees I ever saw stands in Spruce Street, just below Fifth Street, Philadelphia, on the north side, opposite the Baptist church. If you have never noticed it, it is quite worth while to go by that way on purpose to take a look at it. Its branches grow east and west, and north and south, and up and down, and in every possible direction. Yet there was a time when all those crooked-looking branches might have been unbended and made to grow almost as straight as a yardstick. But who can make them so now? All the people in the world could not do it. They might cut the tree down and break its branches in pieces, but that is all they could do. A tree like that shows us exactly what Solomon meant when he said, "That which is crooked cannot be made straight."

And now we come to the third thing we wish to speak of in connection with our text; and that is, the importance of keeping straight while we are getting educated. Did you ever know a person who had charge of a nursery of young trees? If you did, you might learn some very useful lessons from his example. The great object with him is to keep his trees in proper shape while they are growing. He walks about among them very often, and watches them closely. If he sees one getting crooked, he

THE PHOTOGRAPHER'S. 57

tries to straighten it. If merely bending it with his hands will not keep it straight, then he puts a stake in the ground, and ties the young tree to it, so as to keep it in a right position all the time it is growing. And if the gardener thinks it worth his while to take so much care and pains with the education of a mere *tree*, which, after all, will only last for a few years, how much more careful should we be in educating our *souls*, which are to live for ever and ever !

Did you ever go to a photographer's to have your likeness taken? If you did, you remember how very careful the person who took your likeness was to have you seated properly before he began to take it. He lifted your head up, he set your shoulders back, he altered the position of the hands, three or four times, perhaps, before he could get it to suit. He set a swinging ball in motion for you to look at, so as to have you eyes right; and when everything was arranged just to suit him, he said, "There now; keep just so for a little while, and we'll get a nice picture." Suppose, now, you had shut one eye just at that moment, and kept it shut for two or three minutes: what then? Why, you would have had the likeness of a one-eyed boy or girl. Or suppose you had twisted your face, or screwed up your mouth: why, you would have had a picture of yourself with a screwed-up mouth or a twisted face. Nothing in the world could prevent it. Now, my dear children, this world is God's photograph office; and we are all staying here to have our likeness taken. While we are young the likeness is being taken of what we are to be as men and women. And all the time we are living here the likeness is being taken of what we shall be hereafter for ever. When we become men and women, we may, by great efforts, alter the picture that was made of ourselves in youth. But, when we come to die, the picture that has been taken of us can never, never be altered. However crooked, or awkward, or ugly our features may be, they must remain just as they are. Oh, this is a most important thing to know. And it is a very solemn thing to think about. Every day we live our likeness is being taken for eternity. Let us try to remember this every morning when we rise from our beds. Let us think to ourselves, "I am having my likeness taken for eternity to-day, and I must strive to have a good likeness." And when we are tempted to do anything that is wrong, let us stop and ask ourselves the question, How will this look in that picture of me which must last for ever? And it is not only our words and actions, but our thoughts and feelings, which will appear in these likenesses. Almost every feeling we indulge in our hearts will have its effect upon the countenance. When a person is very angry, you can tell it in a minute from the look of his face. The cheeks flush up, and grow as red as a coal; and the eyes glare and flash like the eyes of a tiger. A face all inflamed with anger would make a very disagreeable picture to look at. And selfishness, fretfulness, unkindness, and meanness will show themselves in the face just as plainly as anger does. And they are just as disagreeable to look at, too. And if we indulge these, or any other wrong feelings, in our hearts or lives, we shall fix the expression of them in the likeness now being made of what we are to be for ever. Whenever we are tempted to give way to these wrong feelings, let us say to ourselves, "No; this will spoil our picture for eternity; this will make a crooked feature in it that will never be made straight. Our likeness is being taken now for eternity. Oh, how important it is that we should keep straight till it is done!"

There is only one other point I would speak upon, in connection with our present text, and that is this:—*How can we get straight and keep straight till our likeness is finished?*

Now, how are we to *get* straight? This is the most important question we can ever have to think about. Remember we are not straight, to begin with. Recollect that the first of our four points was to show that we are all born with crooked or sinful hearts. They must be

CROOKED HEART STRAIGHTENED.

made straight before they can be *kept* straight. How, then, can a crooked, sinful heart be made straight or good? We must take it to Jesus, and pray for Him to take away all that is wicked in it. Jesus is able to do this. But no one else besides Him can do it for us. When David, the king of Israel, was mourning over his own heart because it was so dreadfully crooked and sinful, this was just what he did to get a new heart. He kneeled down and prayed most earnestly to his Saviour to do for him this very thing that we are now speaking of. Would you like to know what he said in his prayer? You can read it all in the fifty-first Psalm. It is a beautiful prayer, and one which we may use for ourselves. In the tenth verse of the Psalm he says, "Create in me a clean heart, O God; and renew a right spirit within me." That is the way, and the only way in the world, to get a crooked heart made straight. Jesus is just as willing to hear such a prayer from a little child now as He was to hear it from King David three thousand years ago, if it is offered as earnestly as David offered it. And He is just as able to answer it now as He was then. He is called *Jesus* for this very reason, because He saves His people from their sins. And He does this by making new hearts in them.

In one of the hymns we sometimes sing is this verse:—

> "Can aught beneath a power divine
> The stubborn will subdue?
> 'Tis thine, Almighty Saviour, thine,
> To form the heart anew."

This, then, is the way to get a crooked heart made straight. It is to take it to Jesus in prayer, and ask Him to do it for you. Every one of us may do this for himself. Every child who feels his heart to be crooked may bring it to Jesus to be made new, just as well as the greatest king or the most learned minister on earth. Jesus said, "Suffer *little children* to come unto Me." And there is nothing for which He so loves to have them come to Him as to bring their crooked hearts to get them straightened.

But when our hearts are *made* straight, *how are we to* KEEP *them straight?* Two things are necessary for this: —*we must get Jesus to help us, and we must help ourselves.* We must get Jesus to help us. Without His help we can do nothing at all in this matter. In this work of cultivating our hearts, God deals with us just as He does with the farmer in cultivating his fields. The farmer must have God's help, and he must help himself, or he will never succeed in raising his crops. He may plough his fields and sow his seed; but if there were no sun to shine on it, and no rain to descend, or no dew to distil upon it, do you suppose that the seed would ever spring up and grow? Never in the world. Now, this is the way in which God helps the farmer. But the farmer must help himself, by preparing the ground and putting in the seed at the right time and in the right way. And if he neglect to do this, the sun may shine ever so brightly, and the rains may pour down ever so plenteously, but will there be any harvest yielded? Of course not. And just so it is in the work of straightening crooked hearts. We must have God to help us, and we must help ourselves. But how will God help us here? By giving us His grace and His Holy Spirit. These are just the kind of help to us, in trying to keep our hearts straight, that the sun and rain are to the farmer in making his crops grow. But how are we to get this help from God? By earnest prayer. God promises in His blessed Word to give His grace and His Spirit, and all that His people need, in answer to their prayers. He says, "Ask, and ye shall receive." Jesus tells us that His Father is "more ready to give these good things to them that ask than parents are to give bread to their children." If you want to keep your hearts straight, then, you must go to Jesus whenever you find anything crooked in them, and beg Him to take it away. Yet He will not help us unless we help ourselves; and all our efforts will do no good unless we have His help. But if we have both, our work will be easy and pleasant, and effectual too. You remember the fable of the waggoner whose team was stalled in the mire. He felt that he never could get it out of himself; so he fell down on his knees, and began to call on his God to help him. But he was told to get up and put his shoulder to the wheel, and whip his horses, and then call for help from heaven, and it should be granted to him. There is a great deal of truth in this fable. God only helps those who help themselves. He does so in reference to the body and the things of this world, and He does just the same in reference to the soul and the things of the world to come. Begin at once, then, my dear children, to find out all that is crooked in your hearts; and, as fast as you find these crooked things out, take them to Jesus and pray Him to make them straight. And when they are *made* straight, seek His help and help yourselves to *keep* them straight. This is the Bible way of straightening crooked hearts. This is the way, the only way, of reaching heaven,—that glorious, happy place where nothing crooked ever enters. May God help us all to walk in this good way now, and may He bring us safe to that blessed place at last, for Jesus' sake! Amen

THE GREAT MAN IN GOD'S SIGHT.

" He shall be great in the sight of the Lord."—LUKE, i. 15.

IF you had never heard these words before, my dear children, I suppose you would be ready, as soon as you heard them, to ask, "Who can this mean? Does it refer to some mighty king or conqueror? Is it David, who killed the giant? or Daniel, who was thrown into the lion's den? Or is it some great soldier, like Alexander, or Julius Cæsar, or Napoleon, that is intended?" No; it is none of these. It is nobody like them that is spoken of here. Our text refers to John the Baptist. And who was John the Baptist? He was the son of a poor priest. He was very poor himself. He was born in a little village among the hills of Judea. He lived in the wilderness, and was never heard of, out of his own family, till he grew to be thirty years old. Then he began to preach in the neighbourhood of Jerusalem. He continued his labours as a preacher for about twelve months. One day he preached a sermon which offended Herod, the king of Judea. Herod became very angry with him, and put him in prison. There he was kept for a while, and then he was beheaded. This was the history of John the Baptist. And yet, before his birth, the angel Gabriel was sent from heaven to tell the father of John that he was to be a great man in the sight of God. Perhaps some of you are ready to say, "Why, this seems very strange; we don't see anything so very great in the life of John the Baptist." I dare say

THE GREATNESS OF BIRTH. 63

a good many people have thought so. But we must bear in mind that there are two kinds of great men. Some are great in the sight of men, and others are great in the sight of God. There is a wonderful difference between these two kinds of greatness. Now, let us consider three questions.

The first is: What makes people great in the sight of men?

The second is: What makes people great in the sight of God?

And the third is: Why is it better to be great in God's sight than in man's sight?

Our first question is: *What makes people great in the sight of men?* Several things do this; but *birth*, or *money*, or *talents*, are the chief things which give this kind of greatness. Some people are considered great simply on account of their *birth*. They happen to be born of parents who occupy a distinguished place in society. We all heard a great deal of talk when a son was born to Louis Napoleon, the Emperor of France. For a long time the newspapers were filled with accounts of the wonderful preparations that were made to celebrate his birth. He was to be called the King of Algiers. He was to be rocked in a silver cradle. When he was born, guns were fired, bonfires were kindled, illuminations were held, bells were rung, flags were waved, and all Paris, if not all France, was in a perfect tumult of excitement. One might have supposed that *that* unconscious baby was really the greatest person ever born into this world. It was a great baby in the sight of men. And yet there was nothing but his birth to make him great. No doubt many a baby was born that same day, in humble life, perhaps in some garret or hut, that will really be a great deal more useful to the world than that emperor's son. Greatness in the sight of men belongs to that child of a palace; but it is greatness which owes its existence to nothing but his birth.

But *money* is another thing on account of which persons

are sometimes considered great in the sight of men. Many people, I suppose, have heard about Stephen Girard. When he was alive he was the richest man in Philadelphia. He was the richest man in this country. He was one of the richest men in the world. He died without leaving any children. But suppose that Stephen Girard had had one only son. And suppose that, instead of leaving his property to the city of Philadelphia, he had left it all to this son. Fifteen millions of dollars to one man; what a rich man he would have been! How much attention would have been paid to that man! How much he would have been honoured and sought after! He might have been an ignorant, stupid, bad man, and yet many persons would have considered him a great man, simply on account of his money. It is a poor, mean, contemptible thing when a person's greatness grows out of his gold. Yet it often does so. Plenty of money is often enough to make people be considered great in the sight of men.

But there is another thing on which this kind of greatness rests the most frequently of all, and that is *talent*. By this is meant *smartness*, or power of mind to do things that other people cannot do, or else to do them better than others can. Here are two little boys, John and William. They both go to the same school, at the same time, and they are both put into the A B C class. John learns the alphabet in three lessons; but William has to go over his again and again, day after day and week after week, for three months, before he knows it. We should say that John had a talent for learning, while William had not. Now, this talent, or power of mind to do things, assumes many different forms, and shows itself in many different ways. Sometimes a man's talent will show itself in a remarkable power to learn languages, as in the case of Sir William Jones. This man learned to read and write twenty-eight different languages. He became one of the most learned men of the age in which he lived. His talents made him a great man in the sight of men. And so it was with Dr Carey, the Baptist missionary to India. When a young man he was a shoemaker. But his heart was full of the love of God; and he resolved to give himself up to the work of preaching the Gospel to the heathen. Some people ridiculed the idea of his becoming a minister. They made sport of him, and called him "the consecrated cobbler." But he paid no attention to their mockery. He gave himself up to the work he had chosen. He had a remarkable talent for learning languages, and he lived to translate the Scriptures into the language of many of the Eastern nations, and thus became the means, as it were, of opening the kingdom of heaven to thousands and thousands of people who would never have heard of Jesus and His salvation but for him. Sometimes a man's talents will lie in a power for painting, as was the case with Benjamin West, the son of a plain Pennsylvania farmer, who became one of the most celebrated painters in the world. Sometimes it will show itself in a power for writing beautiful poetry, as was the case with John Milton and Alexander Pope, who acquired a greatness in the sight of men that will last as long as the English language continues to be read in the world. Sometimes it will show itself in a power to find out curious things about the stars and other heavenly bodies, as in the case of Sir Isaac Newton, who saw an apple fall from a tree one day, and set to studying about it, and found out from it how it is that the stars move so regularly, and a great many other wonderful things which nobody else had ever known before since the world was made. Sometimes this talent will show itself in a power to make curious machinery, as in the case of James Watt, who made the first steam-engine, or of Robert Fulton, who made the first steamboat. These persons will always be considered great in the sight of men on account of their talents. And sometimes, though very rarely, a man's talents will show itself in a power to do *anything* better than other people can do it. This was the case with Washington in America. He had a great talent for everything he was called upon to do. He had a wonderful talent for beating the British, and a wonderful talent for ruling the Americans. He had great talent as a soldier, and great talent as a statesman, and great talent as a farmer, and, better than all besides, he had great talent as a good citizen and a good man. He was great in the sight of men, and great in the sight of God too. But these are the three chief things that make persons great in the sight of men. And this was the first question we were to consider.

And now we come to our *second question*, which is this: *What is it which makes people great in the sight of God?* It is not any of the things which lead to greatness in men's sight. A person may be born of the greatest king that ever lived, and be as rich as Girard was, and have the talents of all the different great men that I mentioned, and yet never be great at all in the sight of God. And then, on the other hand, a person may be born in a garret or a cellar, and never have any money to call his own, and no talent at all to do anything that men call great, and yet may be really great in the sight of the Lord. This was very much the case with John the Baptist. He had neither birth, nor money, nor talents to make him what men would call great; yet God called him a great man. What made him great? And what will make others as great as he was? Now, all that need be said in answer to this question is included in a single word. What an important word it is which leads to such an important result! This word is OBEDIENCE. It was simply his obedience which led to all John's greatness. He did just what God wanted him to do. He did nothing else; and he did this all the time. God wanted John to stay in the wilderness till he was thirty years old, and he stayed there. God wanted him to preach repentance, and he did it. God wanted him to tell Herod of his sin. Now, John knew that Herod was a wicked man, and that he would get very angry with him; yet he went right on and did it. Herod put him in prison and killed him for it; yet John was great in the sight of the Lord. He had nothing but his obedience to make him great.

And if *we* obey God as John did, it will make us great in His sight too. Jesus said to His disciples, "Ye are My *friends* if ye do whatsoever I command you;" that is, if ye obey Me. But Jesus is the Almighty God. He rules and governs more than ten thousand times ten thousand worlds. All the angels of heaven worship Him. It is His *smile* which makes the happiness of heaven. Jesus is so very great Himself that it must make anybody great who is permitted to become His friend. You know, my dear children, how often, when evening comes, the setting sun will shine upon the clouds that are floating in the western sky, and make them look so bright and beautiful that you stand and gaze upon them, and feel as if you never should be tired of looking at them. Before the sun shines on them those clouds look so dark and black that you have no pleasure in seeing them. They owe all their brightness and glory to the sun. And yet the glory which the sun gives them is only in appearance, not in reality. Now, if the sun had the power of making all the clouds he shines on really *be* what they *seem* to be,—if he could actually turn them into glorious, glittering gold,— he would then be doing for the clouds just what Jesus does for all who obey Him and become His friends. He sheds His glory upon and makes them like Himself. He not only makes them *look* great and glorious, but He makes them really *be* so. When David was thinking about all God's goodness to him, he said, "Thy gentleness has made me *great*." All the greatness which people get in men's sight is little and empty; but it is vast, wonderful, substantial greatness which they get who become great in the sight of God. And this is what we have Sunday schools and churches for. This is the end of all our teaching and preaching. The object we have in view in it all is to persuade you to love and serve Jesus. It is to induce you to become the friends of Jesus. And if you do this you will secure true greatness to yourselves. This will make you, like John the Baptist, "great in the sight of the Lord." And this is a great deal better than being great in the sight of men.

And now we come to our *third and last question,* which is: *Why is it better to be great in the sight of the Lord than in the sight of men?* We may answer this question by saying that it is so for *three* reasons. Greatness in God's sight is better than greatness in man's sight, because it is *more useful.* Great men in God's sight are more useful than others by *their example.* Now, the most useful thing that can be done to anybody is to make him a Christian. And whatever is the best help towards making any one a Christian, that is the most useful thing to him. But there is nothing like the influence of a Christian's example to help to make others Christians. And in this way a real Christian is doing good to those about him all the time. A man may be born of a prince, and be very rich and very talented; yet there is nothing in any of these things to make his example useful in the way of which we are now speaking. But when any one is great in the sight of God, as John was, by obedience to His will, he is exerting an influence all the time which tends to make others obey Him too; and thus such a person is more useful by his example than those who are great in the sight of men.

And then by his *prayers,* as well as by his example, such a person is more useful. Suppose a great king had a treasure-house filled with all kinds of good things; and suppose he should give the key of this treasure-house to one of his servants, and should tell him that he might open it whenever he pleased and take out anything that was necessary for his own happiness or that of his friends. What a privilege this would be! How much good this person might do! How very useful he might make himself! But this is just what God does to His people. He has a treasury in heaven which contains everything necessary to our happiness. Prayer is the key that unlocks this treasury. God puts this key into the hands of His people,

A CHRISTIAN'S EFFORTS.

and allows them to use it for themselves or others as there may be occasion. As the hymn says,—

> "Prayer makes the darkened cloud withdraw;
> Prayer climbs the ladder Jacob saw·
> Gives exercise to faith and love,
> Brings every blessing from above."

The prayer of Abraham would have saved Sodom and Gomorrah from being burnt up if ten good people had been found there. The prayer of Moses saved the whole nation of Israel from destruction. The prayer of Elijah brought rain on the land when there had been none for three years and six months. And a great many such instances may be found in the Bible. But every Christian loves to pray, and by his prayers he will be more useful than those can ever be who have not learned to pray.

And then those who love and serve God, and are great in His sight, are more useful than others by their *efforts*, as well as by their example and prayers. You remember, my dear children, when Jesus was on earth, as soon as He called some of His disciples, and they found out who He was, they went right away to tell their friends and relations, and tried to bring them to Jesus too. And just so it is now. As soon as a person becomes a real Christian and finds out what a precious Saviour Jesus is, he will try to persuade others to love and serve Him too. Hence you will find such a person becoming a Sunday-school teacher, or a tract-distributer, or a Bible-reader, or a visitor of the sick. And these are among the most useful things that any one can do. The reason why they are so is because they are means which God has appointed for saving souls from death, and to save a soul is the most useful thing in the world. If you or I could make a world like this we live in, we should feel that we had done some very great thing. Yet Jesus has told us that *one* soul is worth more than a whole world. If we should be the means, therefore, of leading one person to love and serve Jesus, we really do more good than if we could make a world. This is one reason, then, why greatness in God's sight is better than greatness in the sight of men. It is more *useful*.

But it is so, again, because this greatness is *more lasting* than the other. Greatness in man's sight—a greatness that connects itself with birth, or money, or talents merely—will soon pass away; but greatness in God's sight—a greatness that connects itself with our being made good and holy—will *never* pass away. The former of these is like having one's name written on the sand upon the ocean shore, where the next wave will wash it away. The latter is like having one's name chiselled in marble, so that it cannot easily be done away. One of these is like the height which a person reaches who gets on stilts. He may stalk round for a little while high up above others; but pretty soon he must lay aside his stilts, and then he comes down as low as anybody. The other is like the height of one who rises by actually *growing* tall. He will remain to-morrow, and next year, and always, just as tall as he may become to-day. One of these kinds of greatness is like a sky-rocket. It shoots up suddenly into the sky with a great rush and blaze, and then just as suddenly it goes out again in total darkness. Its beauty fades, its brightness disappears, and the blackened stick falling to the earth is all that remains of it. The other is like the star which God has set in the heavens. It shines with a clear, calm, beautiful, steady light. It has been shining so for ages past; it will be shining so for ages to come. And this is just what God Himself compares His people to when He says, "They that be wise shall shine as the brightness of the firmament, and they that turn many to righteousness *as the stars* for ever and ever." Greatness in the sight of God is better than greatness in the sight of men, because it is more lasting.

And then it is so, again, *because it is within the reach of all*. This is not true of greatness in the sight of men, but it *is* true of greatness in the sight of God. Can we all be born of kings or princes? No. Can we all become as rich as Girard was? No. Can we all become great poets like Milton, or great painters like West, or great generals like Wellington, Napoleon, or Washington? No. But may we not all become great in the sight of the Lord as John the Baptist was? Yes, we may. For it was the grace of God which made him what he was, and the same grace will be given to us if we seek it with all our hearts. It is spoken of as "the grace of God which bringeth salvation to *all* men." All may seek it; all may secure it; and all may be made great by it. There was a book published several years ago, which almost everybody read. The name of one of the principal characters described in the book was "Uncle Tom." He is represented as a negro slave in one of the Southern States of America. He is described as a good man, and a great man, although but a poor slave. Some people think there never was such a character among the slaves.* But I dare say a great many such could be found among them. A clergyman, who had spent many years in the West India Islands before slavery was abolished, gave me an account of such a one whom he knew very well. He assured me it was strictly true. He said there was once an insurrection in one of those islands—that is, that some had undertaken to put down the laws and the magistrates, and do just what they pleased. Among other things, they resolved to break up the religious meetings of the slaves in that neighbourhood. These meetings were conducted by an old slave called Uncle Ben. He was a pious, excellent negro, who was respected and loved by all who knew him. He had learned to read, and was a sort of minister among the slaves in that part of the island. The rioters went to the negroes' meeting-house at the time of service for the purpose of breaking it up. It happened that Uncle Ben was not there that day. He was unwell; and one of his friends was conducting the

---

* The original of "Uncle Tom," Mr Josiah Henson, visited Great Britain several times on a lecturing tour, and gave an account each time of the hardships and hairbreadth escapes through which he had passed during his slave life.

meeting. The rioters went in and seized the leader of the service. They led him out of the meeting-house and put him to death without a moment's delay. They struck off the poor fellow's head and set it on a pole, and then went round to the different plantations to terrify the poor negroes by this bloody sight of the head of their praying leader. In the course of their march they came to Uncle Ben's cabin. They halted at the door and sent some one to fetch him out. When he appeared, the leader of the mob pointed to the bleeding head on the pole, and asked, " Do you know that head, Uncle Ben?" "Yes, massa," says Ben; "I knows him." "Well, Ben, that's what he's got for his praying. And if you don't stop praying that's just what you'll get. The next time we catch you praying we'll do just the same with your head."

While this was going on a great number of the slaves had gathered round, who looked with intense interest on this scene. They were the fellow-slaves of Uncle Ben, and most of them members of his church. Ben gazed upon the head of his friend. Then he looked the leader of the mob full in the face, and said, " Massa, you mean dat?" "To be sure I do," said the man; "and if you wish to keep your head upon your shoulders you'll give up praying at once." Ben turned to his fellow-slaves in a moment, and said, "Bredren, let us pray." Then he knelt down in the presence of those fierce lawless men, and poured out his soul in prayer. He prayed that God would pardon their sin, and show them the evil of their ways, and change their hearts by His grace. He prayed that God would give him and his fellow-slaves grace to be faithful to their Christian profession, and never by any threats or dangers to be turned away from their duty to Him. When he ceased he rose up and went into his cabin. God's power was on the hearts of those rioters, so that they went away without offering to touch him. Uncle Ben was a great man, although he was but a slave.

Now, look at another instance. A steamboat is making her way through the sparkling waters of Lake

Erie. The pilot at the wheel is old John Maynard. He is a bluff, weather-beaten sailor, tanned by many a burning summer's sun and many a wintry tempest. From one end of the lake to the other he is known by the name of "honest John Maynard;" and the secret of his honesty to his neighbours is his love to God.

The land is about ten miles off, when the captain, coming up from his cabin, cries to a sailor,—

"What's all that smoke there, coming out of the hold?"

"It's from the engine-room, I guess," said the man.

"Down with you, then, and let me know."

The sailor disappeared for a moment beneath, and then returned much faster than he went, and exclaimed, "The hold's on fire, sir!"

The captain rushed down and found the account too true. Some sparks had fallen on a bundle of tow. No one had seen the accident; and now not only much of the baggage, but also the sides of the vessel, were in a smouldering flame.

All hands, passengers as well as sailors, were called together, and two lines being formed, one on each side of the hold, buckets of water were passed and repassed. Filled from the lake, they flew along the line of ready hands, were dashed hissing on the burning mass, and then passed on the other side to be refilled. It seemed for a few moments as if the flames were subdued.

"How's her head?" shouted the captain.

"West-sou'-west, sir," answered Maynard.

"Keep her sou' and by west," cried the captain; "we must go ashore anywhere."

It happened that a draught of wind drove back the flames, which soon began to blaze up more furiously towards the saloon, and the partition between it and the hold was soon on fire. Then long wreaths of smoke began to find their way through the skylight; and, seeing this, the captain ordered all the women forward. The engineer put on his utmost steam; the American flag was run up, with the union down, in token of distress;

and water was thrown on the sails to make them hold the wind. And still John Maynard stood by the wheel, though now he was cut off by a sheet of smoke and flame from the ship's crew.

Greater and greater grew the heat; the engineers fled from the engine-room; the passengers were clustering round the vessel's bow; the sailors were sawing planks to lash the women on; the boldest passengers were throwing off their coats and waistcoats, and preparing for one long struggle for life. And still the coasts grew plainer; the paddles as yet worked well; they could not be more than a mile from the shore, and boats were seen starting to their assistance.

"John Maynard," cried the captain.

"Ay, ay, sir!" said John.

"Can you hold on five minutes longer?"

"I'll try, sir."

Noble fellow! And he *did* try. The flames came nearer and nearer; a sheet of smoke would sometimes almost suffocate him; his hair was singed, his blood seemed ready to boil with the intense heat. Crouching as far back as he could, he held the wheel firmly with his left hand till the flesh shrivelled and the muscles cracked in the flames. Then he stretched forth his right hand and bore the same agony without a scream or a groan. It was enough for him that he heard the cheer of the sailors to the approaching boats, and the cry of the captain, "The women and children first, then every man for himself, and God for us all!" These were the last words he heard. Exactly how he perished was never known. Whether, dizzied by the smoke, he lost his footing in endeavouring to come forward, and fell overboard, or whether he was suffocated and fell into the flames, his comrades could not tell. At the moment the vessel struck the boats were at her side; passengers, sailors, and captain leaped into them, or swam for their lives; and all, save he to whom under God they owed everything, escaped.

THREE THINGS IN JOHN'S EXAMPLE.

We see from these cases, my dear children, that the poorest persons, and those in the humblest positions of life, may become great in the sight of the Lord. Who would not rather be great in the sight of God than in the sight of men? This greatness we may all attain to if we only try aright. But there were three things in John's case that we must remember if we want to succeed. *John began early.* He did not wait till he grew up to be a man before he loved and served God. He began while he was yet a child. And so must we if we wish to be really great in goodness.

And then *John had the Holy Spirit to help him.* When the angel Gabriel told John's father, Zacharias, that God was going to give him a son, he said that he would be "filled with the Holy Ghost from the time he was born." John never would have been good or great in the sight of God without the help of this blessed Spirit; and nobody else ever will either. If you want to be great, as John was, you must get the help of the Holy Spirit as he did.

And then, again, *John gave up everything that was likely to hinder him from becoming great.* We are told that "he drank neither wine nor strong drink." He was a temperate man, not only in drinking, but in eating, and in everything. And so must we be if we would be great in the sight of God. May God help us all to remember these things, my dear children! May He give us grace "to follow John's doctrine and holy life, that we may truly repent according to his preaching; and, after his example, constantly speak the truth, boldly rebuke vice, and patiently suffer for the truth's sake, through Jesus Christ our Lord." Amen.

THE LILY'S LESSONS.

" Consider the lilies of the field."—MATT. vi. 28.

THERE was once a man who was a great writer. He had a wonderful power to tell just what people think and feel; and he had the power to tell these things in a way that nobody else could, so that those who read what he wrote or heard what he said would exclaim, "That is just what I think and just what I feel." Now, this man, when writing once about the pleasantness of being in the country, said he loved to be there because he could

> " Find tongues in trees, books in the running brooks,
> Sermons in stones, and good in everything."

And this is all true, my dear children. Perhaps you never thought of it, but it is still true. It is true there are "tongues in trees;" it is true there are "books in the running brooks" as they flow through the fields and the woods. It is true that there are "sermons in stones;" and every little pebble you pick up by the side of the stream, if you know how to think of it rightly, will preach a sermon to you. It will tell you about the goodness and power of God in a better way than I can do, or any other living preacher. And it is true that there is "good in everything."

And now, dear children, when you go into the country this summer, I hope you will have a right nice time of it in wandering through the sweet fields and woods; but I hope you will not spend all the time in play. See if you cannot find out tongues in the trees, or hear words in the brooks, or find thoughts in the flowers. Yes! every leaf has a tongue, and every little flower. They all tell us of God. They are the thoughts of God. Somebody has said they were the smiles of God. But whatever we may think of this, we know they all have tongues to tell us something. And if we only learn to understand what they teach, how many wise and profitable things may we learn from them!

I remember reading about a missionary who was stationed in a distant country, far away from all his friends and loved ones at home. He had many trials to bear. At first he bore them cheerfully. He loved his work, and was very happy in attending to it. But, after a while, a change took place in his feelings. He lost his trust and confidence in God, and began to think there was no truth in what he had been believing and teaching. He had doubts about the Bible and the truth of God's Word, and even doubted whether there was a God at all who made the world and all things; and in this uncomfortable state of mind he was not fit to preach nor attend to any of his duties.

But once, while going on horseback to preach, and thinking of all these things,—of his unhappy state, and his doubts about the truth of what he was to preach,—his way led him along a thickly-shaded path; and, as he went on, a little leaf dropped from one of the trees over his head, and came shaking, trembling down (you know how the little leaves fall), and lighted right in front of him on the saddle. He picked it up, looked at it, turned it over, and, as the sun was shining through the trees, held it up to the sunlight and saw all the beautiful little veins, looking like a delicate piece of lace or network. He thought, "Yes! that little leaf tells me the Bible is true,—tells me there is a God; for none but a wise, merciful, good, and powerful God could have made a little leaf like that. I am sure it is all true;" and he went on his way rejoicing, feeling happy and thankful.

Now, dear children, didn't that leaf have a tongue for that missionary? Didn't he find a tongue in the tree from which that little leaf fell down? Certainly he did; and if we will only consider the flowers and leaves that God has made, we shall find them *always* telling us about God and good things.

It was in this way, dear children, that our Saviour taught the people wise and good things. Once, when He was walking through the fields, He saw a man sowing, when He began to preach a sermon about sowing the seed. Again, while going along, He saw a shepherd leading the sheep to pasture, when He preached a sermon about the Good Shepherd. And yet again, while walking by the lake, He saw some fishermen in their boats, mending their nets to catch fish, when He preached them a sermon about being fishers of men, or engaging in the ministry. One day, being under a shady vine, and seeing the beautiful clusters hanging down from the branches, He compared Himself to the vine and His people to the branches, and preached a sermon about that. At one time He told the people about the little birds; and here He tells us about the lilies:—" Consider the lilies of the field."

Now, we are going to try to learn from the lilies this afternoon. The lessons we are about to consider are those which the lily teaches.

There are *four* lessons we should all learn from the lily.

In the first place, there is *the lesson of its growth.*

The lily, in its beginning, is a very unpromising plant. It starts out of the earth from an ugly-looking bulb or root, in size and shape something like an onion, so that, without knowing what the lily is, you would never think that anything beautiful could come out of that unsightly and unpromising little root. Nobody would think so. But, children, put it in the ground and cover it up, and then we shall see. God will make the rains and dew come down upon it; He will make the sun shine upon it and warm it, and by-and-by a little sprout will begin to

THE LILY'S GROWTH.

grow, so tender that you could take it with your finger and thumb and destroy it with the slightest nip; and yet it has the power to thrust aside the earth and force its way through the ground until it comes to the surface. Then, when it feels the warm sun and fresh air, it grows faster, sprouts up higher and higher, and by-and-by come the beautiful green leaves, which drink in the dew and rain, and seem to rejoice in the sunshine when it falls upon them. Then the pretty little bud comes out from the beautiful leaves, shows its little head, grows larger and larger, until it bursts into the beautiful white lily.

Now, all the people in the world could not make one of these little bulbs grow up into such a beautiful flower. No: God alone can do it. Yet, dear children, the growth of the lily is just like our own growth. Suppose we take one of these little girls or little boys seven or eight years old. Their eyes are bright like diamonds, and their faces rosy with health and life. God has made them well; their little faces tell it. Suppose I ask you, "What are you made of?" what would you say? "Dust." Yes! dust; you are made of dust! Suppose one of you should die, and we should put you into an iron coffin and bury you in the grave for four, or five, or ten years, and then take the coffin up and open it: what should we find in it? Dust!—a little heap of dark dust, that you or I might take in the hollow of our hand! These bright eyes are dust; these rosy cheeks are dust; these active limbs are dust; these curling ringlets are all, all dust. God has made them grow out of dust. Oh! what wonderful power and wisdom God must have to make these beautiful lilies grow out of this little root, and make these eyes, and cheeks, and hands, and feet, and bodies all grow out of a handful of dust!

What a lesson the growth of the lily teaches! Yes, my dear children, the growth of the lily, and our own growth, both teach us a lesson of the power and wisdom of God.

Now, when you look upon the lilies, or roses, or beautiful flowers of any kind, as you wander in the woods this summer; when you sit beside the pebbly brook or under the shade of the trees, and see a little flower peeping up from among the grass around it, stoop down and pluck it, and think of this text, "Consider the lilies." Consider the flowers, and think what they teach of the power of God and the wisdom of God to make all these beautiful things come out of the dust! Remember, then, dear children, the first lesson: the lesson of its *growth*.

The *second* lesson which the lily teaches us is *the lesson of humility*.

It teaches us the lesson of humility in two things about it: *the position in which it grows, and the attitude which it assumes*.

The lily loves to grow in lonely and retired places. It loves to stay in the background,—to be in the shade. It is the "lily of the valley." You do not find it on the mountain-top, or growing in the streets or garden-walks, but you must go into the retired and shady places; and, when you want to look for its flowers, you won't find them the first thing you see in the garden, but you must go into the corners, and, when you get there, push aside the leaves, and there you will see the beautiful flower, all alone in the seclusion of a shady corner. It is an humble flower, and it teaches a lesson of humility in *the place in which it grows*.

And then its *attitude* shows its humility as well as its position; for when the lily grows up it hangs its head down as though it wanted to hide itself. It does not spread itself out like the proud dahlia or tulip, as much as to say, "Ain't I a beautiful flower?" Oh, no; when the lily gets its full growth, and its beautiful white flowers are formed, it hangs down its head as though it wished to hide its beauty, and felt that it had nothing to be proud of at all,—as though God meant the very form and attitude of this flower should teach us humility. Now, dear children, humility is one of the sweetest things for anybody to have, and especially for boys and girls.

A MISSIONARY'S HUMILITY.

Nothing is more lovely in young persons than to be humble,—to cultivate humility.

You have all heard about Dr Morrison, a missionary to China. As his labour was great and almost too much for one to accomplish, he wanted some one to help him; and he wrote home to the Missionary Society in England to send out another missionary.

When they got his letter, they set to work to inquire among their friends for a suitable young man to go out to China as a missionary to help Dr Morrison. After a while a young man from the country—a pious young man, who loved Jesus Christ—came and offered himself. He was poor, had poor clothes on, and looked like a countryman—rough and unpolished. He went to these gentlemen, was introduced to them, and had a talk with them. They then said he might go out of the room till they consulted with each other about him. When he was gone they said they were afraid the young man would never do to help Dr Morrison; that it would not do to send him as a missionary, as he was but a rough countryman. Finally, they said to one of their number, Dr Phillips, "Doctor, you go out and tell the young man that the gentlemen do not think him fit to be a missionary, but if he would like to go out as *servant* to a missionary, we will send him." The Doctor did not much like to do it; but he told the young man that they did not think he had education enough, and a great many other things necessary for a missionary, but if he would go as a servant they would send him out. Now, a great many would have said, "No, you don't do any such thing; if I can't go as a missionary I won't go at all; you don't catch me going as anybody's servant!" But no, children; he did not say so. He calmly said, "Very well, sir; if they do not think me fit to be a missionary I will go as a servant; I am willing to be a hewer of wood or drawer of water, or to do anything to advance the cause of my heavenly Master." He was then sent out as a servant, but he soon got to be a missionary, and turned out to be the *Rev. Dr*

Milne, one of the best and greatest missionaries that ever went out to any country. All this, my dear children, sprang out of his humility.

One time, in the reign of George III., King of England, there was a learned and a good man who had been appointed Chief-Justice of the country—one of the highest and most honourable offices in England. This gentleman had a son about sixteen years of age, and one evening, as he was about retiring, he called him to his room, and said, " My son, I want to tell you the secret of my success in life. I can give it to you in one word—*humility*. This is the secret of it all; because I never tried to push myself forward, and was always willing to take the place assigned to me, and do the best I could in it. And, my son, if you want to be successful, learn humility."

And humility is a very lovely trait, and beneficial not only to ourselves, as in the case of this Justice, but to others, as I will now show you.

A young preacher once, of the Methodist Church, was sent out on a circuit to preach the Gospel. He was sent, not in the city, but in the country. One evening, as he was going upon his journey to preach, he stopped at the house of a farmer who was also a Methodist. This farmer, though a good man, was sometimes very cross. He had met with some people who deceived him, and professed to be what they were not. When the minister, therefore, came to his house—as he was rather rough-looking and uneducated, though the love of God was in his heart, and he desired to preach the Gospel—he told the farmer what he came for. The farmer was very cold to him, and even said something about being often deceived by people who were not what they seemed to be. "There's my barn," said he; "put up your horse in the barn." He had plenty of servants, and might have sent one of them, the young minister thought; and he was about to mount his horse and go on his way, although it was going to rain. Then he thought he would not: " That is not the way Jesus would have done," he said to himself; so he took his horse to the barn and went to the house. When he came to the front-door the farmer sent one of his servants to take him round to the kitchen; and, when there, he found some very coarse provision spread out for him on a rough, solitary table. He thought it very strange, and the servants in the kitchen thought it strange too, that their master should send the minister to the kitchen. The young man felt much hurt, and thought he could not stand it, and would get his horse and go on again; but he said to himself, "Jesus would not have done so; I will try to be humble like Jesus."

He sat down to eat the bread, and did not complain. After a while he heard the bell ring for prayers, and he went in with the servants to the room and took his place. The farmer read a chapter, and, on getting through, it was very clear he had not made up his mind whether he would pray himself or call upon the minister. At last he called on the young man, and asked him to pray. The minister felt glad to have an opportunity of praying; and when he began he forgot everything but the presence of God, and he poured out his feelings in prayer before Him. His heart was full, and his feelings, which had been wounded by what he had just borne, were relieved by tears. He wept; the servants wept; the people of the family wept; and even the farmer himself wept, and they had a weeping time of it—all kneeling down, and all melted to tears. When they got up the farmer came to the young minister, the tears running down his cheeks, and took him by the hand, and said, "Oh, forgive me, my dear friend and brother, forgive me, and I will pray God to forgive me too, for treating you so unkindly. I do not know what is the matter with me. Satan has been tempting me to do everything that is wrong. I am ashamed of myself for treating you so. I wonder you said nothing cross, and was willing to stay when I sent you to the kitchen." The minister said, "I was trying to do like Jesus, and as He would have done; and I hope you will try to do so too." The farmer took him into his parlour and gave him the best bed and the best room in the house to occupy that night, and pressed him to stay two or three days. He consented to stay the next day, when they had a meeting, got the people together, and the minister preached. That sermon was blessed in the conversion of two or three souls. Two or three of the farmer's family were converted to God, and became useful Christians. Oh, what a blessed thing it was for that farmer's family and for that neighbourhood that this minister understood humility!—that he was an humble-minded man, and had learned the lesson of humility that the lily teaches, and that Jesus teaches!

Jesus is the great lesson of humility. He came on earth to teach us to be humble. He came, not as a full-grown man, but as a little child, to teach us humility. He was born, not in a splendid mansion or a costly palace, but in a stable, and His cradle was a manger. And when He grew up to be a man and went about preaching, He was so poor that He had not where to lay His head—so dependent that women ministered unto Him. He was a servant and not a master. On one occasion, when His disciples were all in a room together, He took a towel and girded Himself. Then He took a basin of water and washed their feet, and wiped them with the towel. He did all this to teach us the lesson of humility.

Now, my dear children, I want you all to learn the lesson of humility which Jesus teaches, and which the lily teaches.

The *third* lesson the lily teaches us is *the lesson of contentment*.

The lily is satisfied with the place in which God has put it. It grows there, and likes it better than any other; and although the roses are out in the middle of the garden, the lily does not fret or envy them; and though the rose-bushes are much larger, the lily is satisfied with being a little plant that can just grow up in the shade, and lets the other plants grow up above it. The lily is contented with its position and size and colour; and although the rose has its beautiful red, and the lilacs and dahlias have their different colours, the lily has only the one beautiful white. Indeed, it is satisfied with its colour, its place, its size, and all that God has made it to be and have.

Ah, my dear children, if we would only learn this lesson, how happy should we be! Take it to your homes, and when you get up in the morning to be dressed, remember the lilies, and if you do not find your bonnet just what you like, be content with it. And if you do not find your coat, your collar, or something else you have to put on exactly what you would wish it, be content with it, and remember the lily. How happy you would make your home, and how much unhappiness you would save yourself!

There was once a good bishop who had a great many things to vex him; but he never murmured; he was always pleasant. Some one said to him, "Well, Bishop, I should like to know what is your secret of always being so happy. You have a great many troubles, trials, and difficulties, but I never see you worried nor hear you complain about them. What is the secret?" "Oh, the secret is, I look up; my object is to get to heaven, which is above. I look around and I see a great many people having worse trials than I have, and I am satisfied with my lot. I look to the graveyard, and see that when I die I am only to occupy a space six feet long and eighteen inches wide, and I am satisfied with what I now have." That was the secret: looking up to heaven, hoping to get there at last, looking around at others who are worse off, and then to the grave, in which we must all soon rest.

Now, children, I have a capital rule to give you about fretting and grumbling,—a very short rule, which it is worth your while to recollect if you want to cultivate contentment. Now, listen, while I tell you this rule, and try to practise it. "*Never fret about what you can't help,*" because it won't do any good. "*Never fret about what you* CAN *help*," because, if you *can* help it, do so. When you are tempted to grumble about anything, ask yourself, "Can I help this?" and if you can't, don't fret; but if you can, do so, and see how much better you will feel.

Oh, remember this little rule! I want all these dear children to begin while they are young to practise it. Before you go to bed to-night think about it: "Never fret about what you can't help, nor what you can help,"—and *fret not at all.*

My dear children, it appears that everybody has trials; and the only way to get along is not to be wishing for what we cannot get, but to learn the lily's lesson of contentment, and be satisfied with what God has given us.

The *last* lesson the lily teaches is *the lesson of its beauty.* Oh, if I only had one here, you could see for yourselves how beautiful it is! There are three things in which its beauty consists: its form, its colour, and its fragrance. It grows into a beautiful rounded flower, and has no sharp edges or corners. Then its colour shows its beauty. It is a beautiful pure white. It is satisfied with one shade, and does not want red, or yellow, or purple, or blue, or pink, but is contented to be a beautiful white lily. Then its fragrance forms a part of its beauty. It perfumes the air, and before you see it you say, "There's a lily about here." You search for it, and trace it by its scent, until you find its little head in all its beauty hidden among the leaves. There is also another thing in which I may say its beauty lies. It is a type of Christ our Saviour. He calls Himself the "Lily of the Valley" and the "Rose of Sharon." The form and colour and fragrance of the lily are all emblems to us of the beauty of Jesus Christ, and of what Jesus will make us if we are His children.

May God give us all grace to be humble and contented! May He help us to learn and practise these lessons! for in so doing we shall find greater happiness and comfort than in anything else.

Now, children, during the summer, when you go into the fields and woods, oh, remember this text, "Con-

THE USE OF THESE LESSONS.

sider the lilies of the field," and learn the lessons of their growth, their humility, their contentment, and their beauty.

My dear children, remember them; don't be satisfied with having them in your *heads*, but try to get them in your *hearts*, and keep them there. Don't be satisfied with *talking* about them, but try and *practise* them, especially these two,—humility and contentment,—which the lily so beautifully teaches. Again, you must begin to practise them *now* while young. It will be better for you than thousands of gold or silver, or the richest fortune you could possibly have, or the greatest luxuries this world can afford.

Pray God to give you grace to be humble and contented, and to learn wisdom from the flowers of the field. When you see or think of these flowers, lift up your thoughts to Him who made them and you; and that glorious Saviour who likened Himself to the lilies will teach you to find beauties in nature and in everything around you.

Remember, then, dear children, the lessons you have heard; and may God bless them to you, and to me, and to us all!

THE GIFT FOR GOD

" My son, give Me thine heart !"—PROV. **xx**iii. 26.

SUPPOSE the angel Gabriel should come down from heaven and stand here before us all, dressed in shining white, with his face brighter than the sun: what a beautiful sight he would present ! And suppose he should take a roll of paper from his bosom, and say he had a list of names that God had given him of fifty girls and fifty boys, and that God wanted all of them to give him something which they had; and suppose he should begin to unroll the paper, and say that he was going to read out the names and tell us what it was that God wanted: how strange we should feel ! Each one would be saying to himself, " I wonder if *my* name is there; I wonder what He wants me to give." And when you heard your name read out, how glad you would feel ! And suppose the angel should say that he wanted you to go home and get what he was sent for that he might take it back with him, how gladly you would go ! how quickly you would run ! how soon you would be back and bring him what he wanted ! No matter what it might be,—if it was your most valuable book, or your favourite plaything, your nicest doll, your new bonnet, or dress, or cap, or coat,—something that you prized most of all that you possessed,—how gladly you would bring it !

But, my dear children, there is no angel here. There is only a man speaking to you; but still it is a minister of God who is speaking, and it is a message from God that he has to deliver. He comes to tell you of something which you have that God wants. Listen to what the text says; it is God who is speaking in the language of the text; it is God who says, " My son, give Me thine heart."

Now, there are two things I wish to talk about in connection with these words.

The *first* is: *What it means to give God our hearts.*
The *second* is: *Why we should give them to Him.*

Now, my dear children, you will notice that God does not ask us to give Him our heads, nor our hands, nor our feet. Is not this strange? Yet there is a reason for it. What do we do with our heads? We think with them. What do we do with our hands? We work with them. What do we do with our feet? We walk with them. But we don't do any of these things with our hearts; that is not what our hearts are for.

Look! here is a little boy who has just returned to his home. He finds his father there, and he hastens to him, and throws his arms around his neck, and says,—

" Oh, my dear father, I do love you with all my———"
what?—why, *heart*, to be sure!

Then what is it that we do with our hearts? Why, we love with them. Yes, my dear children, our hearts were made for this. The heart is the seat or place of the affections.

In a large city like this in which we live there are different places where different things are made. There is the Mint in Chestnut Street, where they make money, and the Navy-yard down in Southwark, where they build ships. And then we have printing-offices, where books are printed; and machine-shops, where engines and locomotives are built; and tailors' shops, where gentlemen's clothes are made; and milliners' shops, where ladies' bonnets are made; and confectioners' shops, where cakes and sweetmeats are furnished; and apothecaries' shops, where medicines are prepared and sold. It would be impossible in a great city to have one place which could furnish all these different things. And so it is in any great manufacturing establishment. There are a great many different things to be done; and these are done, not all together, but each separately, and in a different place. I remember once visiting the Bible-house in the city of New York. This is an immensely large building belonging to the American Bible Society, and where Bibles are made to be distributed all over the world. The whole building is occupied in making Bibles. But of all the multitude of rooms in this great building, each one is occupied with some particular branch of the work. This particular work is done in that one room alone, and nowhere else. There is one room where the paper is moistened and made fit for printing on; and another where the types are set up; and another where the printing is done; and then there is a drying-room, and a pressing-room, and a sorting-room, and a stitching-room, and a binding-room, and a gilding-room, and a finishing-room, and a packing-room. The packing is never done in the printing-room, nor the printing in the packing-room. Each part of the work is done by itself, and kept separate from the rest. And just so it is with our frames, our bodies, and souls. Every man, woman, or child is like a great machine-shop. A multitude of things are to be done, and there is a separate place for the doing of each. There is much seeing to be done, and the eyes are appointed to attend to this. There is much hearing to be done, and the ears are made for this. And then we have the nose for smelling, and the tongue for tasting, and the finger-ends for feeling, and the brain for thinking, and the heart is that part of our frame which has to do with the affections. The heart, you know, is situated right in the centre of the body. When we speak about the heart, we generally place our hand upon the left side, as if the heart were situated just there. But it is no nearer the left side than the right, only we can feel its beatings more distinctly there. Its true place is in the centre of the body. The heart, you know, my dear children, is a hard substance, almost round, and about as large as one's fist. It is divided into four little chambers.

Two of these are employed in pumping the blood into the heart, and the other two in pumping it out. And this pumping is going on day and night, all the time from the moment we begin to live until we die. You can feel this pumping when you lay your hand upon your left side. And if you lie very still at night when you are upon your bed, you can hear it. But is *this* what God wants? Does He wish us to take these real hearts out of our bodies and give them to Him?

Oh, not at all! We read about a nation who used to worship their idol-god in this way. The Peruvians, who lived in South America, used to make offerings to their idols in this manner:—they would drag persons into the temple of their god, and lay them on a table or altar before his image, and take out their hearts and present them, all smoking and quivering, and almost alive, as an offering to him.

But, my dear children, this is not what God wants of us. It is not the literal heart that God wants. He speaks of the heart here in the way of figure as the place where our affections lie; and what He wants us to give Him is not the fleshly hearts out of our bodies, but the affections which are seated in these hearts. When He says, "My son, give Me thine heart," He means, My son, give Me thy love; give Me thy affections; set thy affections on Me; love Me above all things.

This is what the text means when God says in it, "My son, give Me thine heart."

Now, this is the answer to the first question that we proposed,—what it means to give our hearts to God.

The *second* question is: *Why we should give our hearts to God.*

There are *two* reasons for this.

In the first place, we should give our hearts to God *because He has the best right to them.*

He made them for Himself, and they belong to Him. There is a place in our hearts, in our affections, which God designed for Himself to fill or occupy, and nothing else but God can fill that place; and unless God does fill it we never shall be happy, either in this world or in the world to come. And if God made our hearts on purpose that we might love Him with them, surely this is the best reason in the world why we should give them to Him.

Suppose a little girl should spend a holiday in dressing her doll, or a little boy in making a kite or a boat, and just when they were finished,—the doll all dressed, looking very sweetly, and the kite ready to fly or the boat to sail,—some one should come along and take it away with violence: how wrong it would be!

Suppose a gentleman should build himself a beautiful house, and fit it up for his own use, and, just as he was getting ready to move into it and live there, one of his neighbours should get in, and not be willing to let him enter and live in the house that he made for himself: how unjust that would be! That man would have no right to the house. That girl would have no right to the doll, or that boy to the kite or boat. The house, the doll, the kite, or boat, each belonged to the person who had made it, and no one else had any right to it.

What should we call the person who should act in this way? We should call him a robber.

Just so it is, my dear children, with our hearts. God made them for Himself. God desires to keep our hearts. He wishes to come in and dwell in them. He wishes to possess our affections. He desires that we should love Him above all things.

He says in one place in the Bible, "Behold, I stand at the door" [of your hearts] "and knock: if any man hear My voice and open the door, I will come in to him and will sup with him;" but until we are ready to give our hearts to God,—to set our affections on Him,—we are unwilling to let Him come in and dwell in the place He made for Himself to dwell in. Surely this is robbing God!—robbing Him of what He made for Himself—of that which He desires to possess above all things! Oh, how great the wickedness those commit who refuse to give

God their hearts! How many people there are who would be ashamed to rob their fellow-creatures who are not ashamed to rob their God! How many people we find who would not take a pin from one of their fellow-creatures who do not hesitate to take from God all the affection which belongs to Him, and rob Him of those hearts, those affections, which He has made for Himself!

God once sent a prophet to ask the Jewish nation a very singular and startling question (Mal. iii. 8). I think it must have surprised them very much when they heard the question. It was this: "Will a man rob God?"

We are not told what the Jews said to the prophet when they heard his question. I dare say they were ready to exclaim at once, "Why, no! surely nobody can be found guilty of such enormous wickedness!" But before they had time to say anything, God answered the question Himself. He charged the dreadful guilt of this sin upon them. He said, "Yet *ye* have robbed Me, even this whole nation." And then—as if He thought they would ask in surprise, "Why, how have we done this?"—He said, "In tithes and offerings." The *tithes* here spoken of referred to the *tenth* part of all their gains and the produce of their grounds, which God required them to present as offerings to Him. And when they failed to do it, God said they were robbing Him. And if God called them robbers because they would not give him the money or the cattle or grain that belonged to Him, how much more will He consider us as robbers if we refuse to give Him our hearts or affections, which He so earnestly desires, and which He made on purpose that they might be given to Him! Bear this in mind, then, my dear children, that if we do not set our affections on God, and love Him better than anything else, we are robbers; and the worst kind of robbers, too, for we are robbing God. We ought to give our hearts to God because He made them and has the best right to them.

But, again, we ought to give our hearts to God *because He can make the best use of them.*

What sort of hearts are ours when we are born into this world? Are they good or holy? No. What do the Scriptures say of the heart? They say, "The heart is deceitful above all things, and *desperately* wicked."

And what can God do for hearts like these? *He can make them new.* God has promised in His Word (Ezek. xxxvi. 26), saying, "A new heart will I give you, and a new spirit will I put within you; and I will take away the heart of stone, and give you a heart of flesh." When our Saviour was talking with Nicodemus, He said it was by the power of the Holy Spirit that God caused His people to be born again, or to have their hearts made new. And the apostle James (i. 18) tells us what are the means which the Holy Spirit makes use of in accomplishing this work. He says, "Of His own will begat He us with the *Word of truth.*" The truth of His blessed Word—that is, the truth of the Bible—is what the Spirit employs for this purpose. Nobody can tell how this great change takes place. We only know that it is a change which the Holy Spirit works, and that He makes use of the truth of the Bible in order to bring it about. But there is the greatest difference in the world, my dear children, between an old heart and a new heart—between the heart we have by nature and the heart when it is made new by the Holy Spirit.

The old heart is proud, and cross, and disobedient, and selfish, and obstinate. The new heart is humble, and gentle, and kind, and obedient, and holy, and good.

God has given us in His Word a picture of these two hearts. You will find it in the fifth chapter of the Epistle to the Galatians. The natural, or old heart, there is described as being filled with things like these: "Adultery, fornication, uncleanness, lasciviousness, idolatry, witchcraft, hatred, variance, emulations, wrath, strife, seditions, heresies, envyings, murders, drunkenness, revellings, and such-like." But the renewed heart is represented as being filled with the fruits of the Spirit, which are these:

THE HEART CLEANSED. 95

"Love, joy, peace, longsuffering, gentleness, goodness, faith, meekness, temperance." What a contrast between these two hearts!

It will be better for us, my dear children, to have our hearts made new than to possess thousands of gold and silver; but none can make these wicked hearts new but God Himself; and it is for this reason He desires us to give our hearts to Him that He may make them new.

But, again, God will make our hearts clean and holy as well as new. This is another reason why we should give them to Him. No heart ever can be made clean till it is first made new. What a sad thing it is to have a heart that never has been cleansed! What would you think of a boy who had lived till he was twelve or fourteen years old and never had his face washed? How frightful he would seem! And yet, my dear children, how much worse it is to have a heart that has never been washed or made clean!—a heart all defiled by sin, and which has been getting worse and worse every day. But how many such hearts there are! and they never can be washed and made clean until we bring them to God that He may cleanse them. And the way in which God cleanses wicked hearts and makes them holy is by His Word. We read in one place in the Bible that it is "with the washing of water by the Word" that He cleanses wicked hearts and makes them pure and holy. The meaning of this is, that just as we wash our hands or our clothes when they are dirty, and make them clean in water, so by His Word—the water of His truth—does God cleanse sinful hearts and make them pure. Let me give you, now, an illustration of what I mean by this.

"A clergyman was once walking near a brook, when he observed a woman washing wool in a stream. This was done by putting it in a sieve, and then dipping the sieve into the water repeatedly, until the whole became white and clean.

"He entered into conversation with the woman, and,

from some expression she used while she was speaking, he asked her if she knew him.

"'Oh, yes, sir,' she replied; 'and I hope I shall have reason to bless God through eternity from having heard you preach some years ago. Your sermon was the means of doing me great good.'

"'I rejoice to hear it,' said the clergyman. 'Pray, what was the subject?'

"'Oh, sir, I cannot recollect that, my memory is so bad.'

"'Well, how then can the sermon have done you so much good if you don't remember even what it was about?'

"'Sir,' said the woman, 'my mind is like this sieve. The sieve does not hold the water; but, as the water runs through, it cleanses the wool. So my memory does not retain the words I hear, but as they pass through my heart, by God's grace, they cleanse it. Now I no longer love sin, and every day entreat my Saviour to wash me in His own blood, and cleanse me from all sin.'"

Thus it was that this good woman had her heart cleansed "with the washing of water by the Word."

Surely, then, dear children, this is a good reason why we should give our hearts to God,—because He can make the best use of them: He can make them *clean*.

But God will not only make our hearts new and clean; He will also make them happy. And surely this is a good reason why we shall give them to Him. We never can be happy until our hearts are made new. Suppose your arm was broken, or out of joint: could you ever have any comfort in using it while in that position? Of course not. The more you used it the more uncomfortable it would make you feel. You must get the bone set, or the joint replaced, if you ever wish to use it again with comfort. And just so it is with our hearts. Until they are renewed by God's grace we can have no more comfort, no more enjoyment, with them, than we could with a broken or a disjointed limb. And we never shall find any real happiness or comfort until these hearts are renewed; and it is because God knows this so well that He desires us to bring our hearts and give them to Him.

Now, God has told us, my dear children, what He wants of us. He has told us whom He wants it of. He wants it of each one of you.

Let me, before closing, ask you the question, Will you give God your heart? Will you begin to-day and pray for Him to give you the help of His Holy Spirit, that your heart may be made clean and new, and you may find that happiness and peace which can only be found by those who know and love Him?

There is a very sweet hymn in the Sunday-school Hymn-Book, which any one may use as a prayer who desires to obtain this greatest of all blessings that we can ask or God can give. It is this:—

> " Oh for a heart to praise my God,—
> A heart from sin set free;
> A heart made clean by Thy rich blood
> So freely shed for me.
>
> " A heart resigned, submissive, meek,
> My great Redeemer's throne;
> Where only Christ is heard to speak,
> Where Jesus reigns alone.
>
> " An humble, lowly, contrite heart,
> Believing, true, and clean;
> Which neither life nor death can part
> From Him that dwells therein.
>
> "A heart in every thought renewed,
> And full of love divine;
> Perfect, and right, and pure, and good,—
> A copy, Lord, of Thine."

May God give to each of us such a heart as this, for Jesus' sake. Amen.

THE WONDERFUL LAMP.

" Thy Word is a lamp unto my feet."—PSALM cxix. 105.

THE Psalm in which these words are found is the longest chapter in the Bible. It is divided into twenty-two parts, and contains one hundred and seventy-six verses. The shortest chapter in the Bible is the next but one before this—namely, the one hundred and seventeenth Psalm. This contains only two verses. Now, it is worth remembering that the longest and the shortest chapter in the Bible are found so close together. This hundred and nineteenth Psalm is remarkable, not only for its length, but for other things also. It is all written about the Bible. The great object of it is to show what a wonderful and excellent book the Bible is. And this Psalm is remarkable also for the many different names it applies to the Bible. There are no less than *ten* different words made use of in this Psalm to signify the Bible. These are: *law, commandments, testimonies, statutes, judgments, word, precepts, ordinances, way, truth.*

And out of all these one hundred and seventy-six verses there is only one which does not contain one or other of these names of the Bible. Read over this Psalm, verse by verse, and see if you can find more than one verse in which some one of these ten names of the Bible does not occur. Every one of these hundred and seventy-six verses, except the hundred and twenty-second, has something to say about the Bible.

Now, our text is the hundred and fifth verse of this Psalm. And which of these ten names of the Bible is found here? "Thy *Word*." And what does it say of this Word? "Thy Word is a lamp unto my feet." Here the Bible is compared to a lamp. The object of a lamp is to give light. And light is needed by those who are in the dark. And God tells us that this is just our condition here in this world. He says that "darkness covers the earth, and gross darkness the people." This does not refer to the outward or natural world which we see with our bodily eyes. No; for there we have the glorious sun to give light by day, and the moon and stars, in all their beauty, to give light by night. But it refers to the inward or spiritual world—to the state in which our souls are. In the Bible darkness means ignorance; and when it speaks of the people of the world as being in darkness, it means that they are in ignorance respecting God and heaven and the things which belong to salvation. And because the Bible gives us all the light we have on these matters it is called "a lamp." "Thy Word is a lamp unto my feet." God has hung out this blessed lamp in a dark, dark sky; and its heavenly light shines calmly and sweetly down on multitudes of poor, wretched wanderers, who are groping their way amidst all the horrors of midnight gloom and darkness. And while we are thinking on this subject there are two questions that it will be well for us to consider.

The *first* is: *What sort of a lamp is the Bible?*

The *second* is: *What should those who have it do with it?*

Now, there is one word which contains all that need be said in answer to the question, What sort of a lamp is the Bible? and this is the word *wonderful*. The Bible is a wonderful lamp. Almost everybody has heard the Arabian story of Aladdin's wonderful lamp. The story says that this lamp was given to Aladdin by a magician. When the owner of this lamp wanted anything, all he had to do was just to rub the lamp, and instantly the thing that he wanted would be all ready for him. Plenty of money, splendid houses, beautiful carriages and horses, or anything else, could be had in a moment by a simple rub upon the lamp. This *was* wonderful indeed; but I need not tell you there is not a word of truth in it. There never was such a lamp. And even if there had been, the Bible is more wonderful still than that. I would rather have the Bible and the happiness which it brings than ten thousand such lamps as the Arabian story tells of, although every word said of them were true. Why, one of the very worst things that could possibly happen to any of us would be to have our own way, and be able to get everything that we wanted. We should make ourselves perfectly miserable, and ruin ourselves in a short time, as sure as we are alive. The blessed thing about the Bible is that it promises only those things which are really good for us; and these it not only *promises* but *secures* to us. It is a wonderful lamp. But how is it so? What is there about this lamp that makes it wonderful? There are three things about it which are wonderful. It is *wonderful for the* LIGHT *it sheds; wonderful for the* COMFORT *it yields; and wonderful for the* SAFETY *it affords.*

The Bible is a lamp that sheds *wonderful light.* And the light which shines from this lamp is wonderful in several respects. It is wonderful *for the length of time* during which it has been shining. Most lamps only burn for a few hours at a time, and then go out. But this lamp has been shining for almost six thousand years. It was lighted in the Garden of Eden. When Adam sinned, he brought that darkness on the world of which we have before spoken. The first promise which God gave him about the Saviour who was afterwards to come was like kindling one little thread in the wick of this lamp. And then, as other parts of the Bible were written, the lamp burned brighter and brighter, till Jesus came and the New Testament was finished. And now for near two thousand years this lamp has been fully lighted and burning all the time. It is a wonderful lamp when you think of the length of time during which it has been shining.

It is wonderful, also, *for the distance to which it shines.* Most lamps, you know, will not shine very far. If you want to see clearly by a lamp, you must go pretty close to it. You can see its light, indeed, for hundreds of yards; and if it is lifted up very high it may be seen even at the distance of several miles. The lamps on some lighthouses can be seen as far as twenty or twenty-five miles. Yet even this is a very trifling distance. The Bible—God's wonderful lamp—shines all the way from heaven to earth. We think it wonderful to have the light of the sun come to us from a distance of ninety-five millions of miles: and so it is. But the light of this lamp shines farther still. Nobody knows how far it is to heaven. But though we cannot measure the distance, yet in the light of this lamp we can see into heaven. It shines so clearly that when we look steadily in its light the pearly gates and golden streets and crystal streams of heaven may be distinctly seen. And not only from heaven to earth does this lamp shine, but from one end of the earth to the other its light is reaching. It is shining now across the widest oceans, and over the highest mountains, and into the darkest corners of the earth. Oh, it is a wonderful lamp *for the distance to which it shines!*

And then it is wonderful also *for the power with which it shines.* Some lamps burn so feebly that the least puff of wind will blow them out. If you want to carry one of them about, you must put your hand before it and go very carefully, or you will be left in the dark. And then, again, if the air is not pure, you often find that lamps will not burn. Sometimes, when people are going down into wells or other deep places, where the air has become impure, the lamps they carry with them go out in a moment. But it is very different with God's wonderful lamp. This shines with so much power that no tempest that ever beat, no wind that ever blew, has been able to put it out. Satan and wicked men hate this lamp, and have tried all they could to stop its shining, but in vain. They have raised storms of fierce persecution; and fire, and sword, and chains, and dungeons have been employed to stop men from reading and circulating the Bible, but they have never succeeded. They have never been able to put out this wonderful lamp or stop it from shining. And as no wind is strong enough to blow it out, so no atmosphere is impure enough to put it out. It has been carried down into the darkest mines, the deepest pits, the foulest dens on the earth, and it has kept on shining there with a clear, steady light, till the darkness was all dispelled and the impurity all removed. And when we think of all these things,—of *the length of time* during which it has been shining, of *the distance through* which and *the power* with which it shines,—we see how truly it may be called a wonderful lamp. It is wonderful *for the light which it sheds.*

But it is wonderful, also, *for the* COMFORT *which it yields.* This lamp yields comfort to people *under the trials of life;* and it yields comfort *in the prospect of death.* There are trials numerous and great to be passed through in life. Whether we are rich or poor, learned or unlearned, we shall find trials which must be passed through; and there is nothing like the Bible—God's wonderful lamp—to give comfort under them. You know there is a hymn which says,—

> " 'Tis religion that can give
> Sweetest pleasure while we live;
> 'Tis religion must supply
> Solid comfort when we die."

Look at Daniel. He was a great man, a wise man, an honourable man. Next to the king, he held the highest position in a nation that was then the mightiest on the face of the earth. But wicked men formed a plot against him. He was falsely accused of being unfaithful to his king and country. He was dragged, as it were, in an instant from his home and his honours. He was hurried away, as it was supposed, to a cruel and disgraceful death. The dark den of hungry lions was opened, and he was thrust into it. But, fierce as those untamed beasts were, they acted with the gentleness of lambs to him. Their mouths were closed, their violence was restrained, by an unseen but mighty power, and they hurt him not. Still, Daniel's position was one of great trial. But he had God's Word to think of. In the darkness of that dreadful den this wonderful lamp was shining in upon Daniel's mind, and he found comfort from it.

Or look at Paul. God had sent him to preach the Gospel. He was going about telling everybody, as he had opportunity, what a glorious Saviour Jesus is, and what great blessings He bestows on all who love and fear Him. But there is a wicked ruler who dislikes to have Paul preach of Jesus. He bids him stop his preaching. Paul will not do this. Then the ruler sends an officer to take him. He orders him to be beaten with rods on his bare back till the flesh is torn and mangled, and the blood flows down in streams from the cruel wounds. Then he is loaded with chains and thrust into a wretched dungeon. Ah, what a trial was that! And how did he bear it? Did he pass the night in crying and groaning over his hard lot? No, indeed. He had God's wonderful lamp with him, and it shone so brightly into his heart and made him so happy that he forgot his mangled, bleeding back; and, as if it was a palace instead of a prison that he was occupying, he sang out the gladness of his heart in psalms and hymns till all the prisoners heard him.

But here is a case from our own times. There is an old man who is a cripple. He lives all alone in a poor, miserable hovel. It is so old and shattered that the wintry winds sweep freely through it. The roof is so out of repair that the melting snows and drenching rains come dripping down in every part except one little corner, which is occupied by the poor cripple's bed of straw. We can hardly think of any situation more wretched and uncomfortable than this. Yet that poor cripple is a real Christian. He loves Jesus, and has a hope of heaven. Would you like to know how he feels in that lonely and cheerless hut?

Well, a Christian friend and neighbour is going in to make a morning call. It is a raw, cold December day. The visitor opens the door, and says to the poor sufferer, "Well, John, how do you do this morning?"

"Oh, sir," he replies, "I am sitting under His shadow with great delight, and His fruit is sweet to my taste." He meant to say by this that he felt the presence of his Saviour, and that this gave him peace and joy amidst all his poverty and pain. God's wonderful lamp was shining in that lowly hovel, and the poor sufferer living there was comforted by it under the trials of life.

But we need comfort *in the prospect of death* as well as under the trials of life; and this wonderful lamp can give it to us here also. It is a solemn thing to die—to bid farewell to all the familiar scenes of earth—to be separated from all the dear friends we have known and loved here—to lie down in the silent grave and moulder into dust—to enter upon the awful and untried scenes of the eternal world—to stand before the judgment-seat of Christ, and have our condition fixed in happiness or misery for everlasting ages: oh, there is something unspeakably solemn in all this! Who can think of it and not feel his spirit awed within him? Ah! we need comfort in the prospect of death more than we can possibly need it at any other time. And we *must* have it, too, or we shall be badly off indeed. Yet there is nothing that can give us real, substantial, satisfying comfort, except the Bible.

This wonderful lamp was lighted on purpose that it might shine on the darkness of the grave. When it *does* shine, there is comfort in the prospect of death; when it does not shine, there is none. Here is a striking illustration of this. Two Hindoos are dying. One of them is still a heathen; he is without this lamp. The other is a Christian; he has it. Now, mark the difference between them. The heathen Hindoo feels that death is approaching fast. He sends for the Brahmin, his priest, and asks him, with great eagerness, "What will become of me when I die?" "At your death," said the Brahmin, "your

THE COMFORT OF THE BIBLE.

spirit will enter the body of some reptile, and live there a long period of time." "And when that is over what will become of me?" asked the dying man again. "Then," said the Brahmin, "you will pass into the body of some animal for another long period." "And what then?" asked the poor man. The Brahmin led him through a long series of changes, reaching over some thousands of years. At every step in the progress he was met by the earnest inquiry of the dying man, "And what then?" He felt that thousands of years were as nothing to eternity. The Brahmin got to the end of all his changes, and still the cry met him, *What then?* But he could not answer it. He had nothing more to say; and the poor dying heathen, without hope or comfort, was compelled to take a leap in the dark, and find out the answer to his question in his own sad experience. God's wonderful lamp had never shone upon him to give him comfort in the prospect of death, and therefore he could find none.

But another Hindoo is about to die. He is a young man connected with a mission-school. There he has learned to read the Bible, and it has taught him the way of salvation. He feels that his last hour has come. He calls one of his friends to his bedside, and, with a countenance beaming with peace and joy, he exclaims, "Sing, brother, sing!" "What shall I sing?" asks his companion. "Sing of salvation through the blood of Jesus. Sing, Thanks be to Him who giveth us the victory through our Lord Jesus Christ;" and then he sank back upon his couch and died. He *had* this wonderful lamp. It had been shining in upon his soul, and its clear shining gave him comfort in the prospect of death.

But this lamp is wonderful *for the* SAFETY *which it affords*. Persons who have to go into coal-mines are exposed to many dangers. One of these arises from a particular kind of gas which is sometimes found there, and which, the very moment it comes in contact with the flame of a lamp or candle, explodes like gunpowder, burning and destroying all persons within its reach. Hundreds of lives have been lost in this way. Some years ago a wise and good man, whose name was Sir Humphry Davy, invented a lamp for the purpose of guarding against the danger of explosion from this gas. It had fine wire gauze arranged round the flame of the lamp in such a way that it would give notice to the miners of the presence of this dangerous gas, and, at the same time, keep the flame of the lamp from touching it till they escaped from the danger. It is called Davy's safety-lamp, and has proved a great comfort and blessing to miners. It has saved a great many hundred lives.

Now, this world is like a great coal-mine, and all its inhabitants are like miners. The sins that abound here are like this dangerous gas, and, when they come in contact with our evil passions, violent explosions are often produced, and great damage is done. We need a safety-lamp to show us where the dangers lie, and help us to escape from them. And just such a lamp we have. The Bible is a safety-lamp which God has invented for this very purpose. If we carry it with us as we move about in this great mine, and use it carefully, it will afford us entire safety. It will always warn us when danger is nigh, and show us how we may escape it. This is just what our text means when it says, "Thy Word is a lamp unto my feet." It is a wonderful lamp. It is wonderful for many things, but for nothing more than for the safety it affords to those who use it rightly. Such persons are said to be "under the shadow of God's wings," and "in the hollow of His hand." What a position of safety this is! This was the position which David occupied when he said, "The Lord is my light and my salvation; whom then shall I fear? the Lord is the strength of my life; of whom shall I be afraid?" He knew that an eye which never slumbers was watching over him, and that an arm which never wearies was stretched out for his defence. And this is just as true of us as it was of David if we are walking by the light of this wonderful lamp. Then the words spoken in Psalm cxxi. 5-8 refer to us, and show the safety we enjoy: "The Lord is thy keeper; the Lord is thy shade upon thy right hand. The sun shall not smite thee by day, nor the moon by night. The Lord shall preserve thee from all evil: He shall preserve thy soul. The Lord shall preserve thy going out and thy coming in from this time forth, and even for evermore." And when we think of the light which this lamp sheds, of the comfort which it yields, and of the safety which it affords, we see how truly it may be called a wonderful lamp. This answers our first question: What sort of a lamp is the Bible?

The second question can receive a much shorter answer. This question is: *What should those who have this lamp do with it?* They should do two things with it: *they should use it themselves, and they should send it to others.* We should use this lamp ourselves. This is what it is given to us for. We all have need to use it. It is shining about us, and into our hearts, on purpose that we may see the greatness of our sins, and then come to Jesus to get rid of them. This wonderful lamp can do us no good unless it shows us the way to Jesus, that we may learn to love and serve Him. We may as well be without it—nay, we had much better be without it—than fail to make a right use of it. *To neglect to use this lamp aright is the greatest sin we can commit.* We shall be condemned to everlasting destruction for this very thing. Jesus said, when He was on earth, "This is the condemnation" (that means, this is the thing for which men will be condemned), "that light is come into the world, and men love darkness rather than light, because their deeds are evil." Then let us, my dear children, use this lamp to find out the way to heaven; and, when we see that way, let us strive to walk in it. This is the right use to make of this lamp for ourselves.

But then we must send it to others as well as make a right use of it ourselves. There was a fisherman once, whose hut was situated on a high and rock-bound coast. Near by was a snug cove, with a smooth sandy beach, where he was accustomed to draw up his little boat, and from which he went forth day by day to engage in his toilsome occupation on the waters of the stormy sea. One day he went out as usual to spend the day in fishing. He toiled on with encouraging success till towards the close of the afternoon; when, looking up to the sky, he saw threatening signs of an approaching storm. Immediately he hauled up his lines, resolving if possible to reach his home before the gathering tempest should burst upon him. But he had a long distance to go, and the wind was ahead, and the sea was rough, and the storm came on fast, and the day was almost gone. Yet with a brave and trusting heart he turned the bow of his boat in the right direction, and began to row towards home. Right manfully did he bend upon his oars, and his boat flew rapidly over the white-capped billows. But darker and darker grew the heavens above him, and soon all trace of daylight had disappeared. The outline of the coast had faded from his view, and he could no longer see any of those well-known landmarks by which he was accustomed to direct his course. He went as near the coast as he could without being dashed against its jagged rocks. And then he rowed on till he was exhausted; but no sign of his hut or of the little cove near by could he discover. The storm raged fiercer, and the night grew darker. Hope died away within him, and death stared him in the face. He expected every moment that his frail boat would be swallowed up in the stormy waters. But just then a faint ray of light met his eye. It renewed his strength. He rowed on more heartily. Very soon he found that it proceeded from the window of his own little hut. It guided him to the cove he was accustomed to enter. He drew his boat up safely on the sand, and, grateful for his own deliverance, before he went to bed that night he trimmed the lamp and filled it with oil, and set it in the window of his humble dwelling, that its friendly light might shine out upon the stormy sea, and perhaps guide some other tempest-tossed voyager to a place of safety. And as long as he lived he continued this practice. It was very proper that he should do this. He made a right use of the lamp himself, and then he tried to extend the benefit of it to others. And this is just what we should do. We *have* God's wonderful lamp. It is shining all about our path. It shows us how we may sail over life's stormy sea so as to reach the haven of enduring rest and safety at last. But there are multitudes of our fellow-creatures who are tossed on this tempestuous sea without a single ray of light to guide their way. What is our duty? Should we not send this wonderful lamp to them? This is all they need. It is abundantly able to guide them to the only place where they can find safety. And when we present our offerings to the missionary cause, when we give our money to send the Bible to the benighted heathen, and when we pray to God to bless our offerings, then we are holding up this wonderful lamp, that those who are in darkness may see its light, and follow its guidance, and be happy for ever. There are two things, my dear children, that you should earnestly pray for. One is that God may give you grace to make a right use of this lamp yourselves; and the other is, that He would help you to do all you can to send it to others. When Jesus was on earth, He said to the people, "While ye have the light, walk in the light, lest darkness come upon you." And He says the same to us. If we neglect to use this lamp properly ourselves, we commit a great sin, and expose ourselves to great danger. And so we do if we neglect to send it to others. For there is a passage of Scripture which says, "To him that knoweth to do good, and doeth it not, to him it is sin." May God enable us " both to perceive and know what things we ought to do; and also give us grace faithfully to fulfil the same," for Jesus' sake! Amen.

THE CHILD'S FORTUNE TOLD.

" Even a child may be known by his doings."—PROV. XX. 11.

THERE are many different ways in which we may know a person. Sometimes we know persons *by sight*. Almost every day in the week, as I pass by the Pennsylvania Hospital, standing against the wall at the corner of Eighth and Spruce Streets, Philadelphia, I see a poor blind coloured man begging and offering matches for sale. I can see him half a square off as I go up and down the street. And if I should see him anywhere else I could tell him in a moment. I know him *by sight*. But where he lives, or whether he has any family, or what sort of a man he is, I cannot tell. I *only* know him by sight. Sometimes we know a person *by name*. Everybody in this country knows the President of the United States by name, though hundreds of thousands of people have never seen him. In the same way almost everybody knows Barnum, the great showman, though very few would know him by sight if he should appear before them. And sometimes we know persons *by description*. If you should read an advertisement of a person who had committed a robbery, in which he was represented as having red hair, being light-complexioned, cross-eyed, with a large wart on his nose, short of stature, and limping on his left foot, although you had never seen the man before, yet, from reading this account of his appearance, you would know him from *description* as soon as you saw him. And then, again,

A CHILD KNOWN BY HIS TEMPER.

persons are known by their *actions;* that is, by certain things that they have done. In this way we all know Noah as the man who built the ark. We know Moses as the man who led the Israelites out of Egypt and through the wilderness. So we know David as the man who killed the giant; and Daniel as the man who was thrown into the lion's den. And so everybody knows Christopher Columbus as the man who discovered America; and George Washington as the man who saved his country; and Benedict Arnold as the traitor who basely betrayed it. And when we read history we learn to know the character of the different persons spoken of by the things they have done. And this is the way of knowing persons that Solomon speaks of in our text. It is not by *sight*, nor by *name*, nor by *description;* but by *actions*. And *children* may be known in this way as well as grown persons. The wise man tells us here that "even a child may be known by his doings."

Now, there are *two* questions to be considered in connection with this text.

The *first* is: *What is meant by " doings" here ?*

The *second* is: *What may be "known" of a child in this way?*

Now, I suppose, when Solomon used the word "doings" here in reference to a child, he meant to speak of three things: namely, *the tempers he indulges; the habits he forms;* and *the company he keeps.*

The *tempers* indulged by every young person constitute part of those *doings* by which he may be known. We all know what *temper* means. It is a word we use to express the kind of feelings we have towards those who are about us. And our tempers have very much to do with making up our characters. Sometimes we look at persons or things through something which makes them appear very different from what they really are. If I look at you through a piece of green glass, you *appear* to be green. And if I look at you through a red piece, you will look red. But this does not prove that you *are* green or red, does it? Of course not. It only proves that I am looking at you and judging of you in a wrong way. But when we look at persons and judge of them through their tempers, we are sure to be right. Then we see and know just what they are. We are all just what our tempers make us. Now, there is as much difference in the tempers of children as there is in the colour of their hair or their eyes, or in the complexion of their countenances. Some children have *cross* tempers. If you speak to them, you are sure to get some sharp, surly answer. They snap and snarl like some ill-natured dog, whose delight is to be as ugly as he can. If you ask them to do the smallest favour, you are sure to be refused, and that, too, in a rough, ungracious manner. Other children have *kind* tempers. They always have something pleasant to say when they are spoken to. They are ready to do everything in their power to accommodate others. They are always striving to make those about them comfortable. They are like little sunbeams, and diffuse a cheerful, happy light wherever they go.

Some children have *fretful* tempers. They are all the time finding fault with something or other. They fret about the weather. It is either too hot or too cold, too wet or too dry. They fret about their clothes. Here is one of these fretters getting dressed. Just listen to him a moment. He takes up his coat. "Such a looking coat!" he murmurs. "Who ever saw the like? About half a mile too big!" *Observe, fretters never tell the truth.* And so he goes on with everything he takes up. His stockings are too thin, and his shoes too thick. One thing is too long, and another too short. One is too tight, and another too loose. These children fret about their *food*, too, as well as their clothes. It is either done too much or not done enough. It is either too coarse or too fine, or too something or other that must be complained of.

Other children, again, have *patient* tempers, the very opposite of these. They never fret about the weather;

PATIENT AND SELFISH TEMPERS.

because they feel that God, who sends it, knows better than they do what kind to send, and what *He* sends must be best. They never fret about their clothes, because they know that hundreds of people are wearing clothes much worse than theirs. And they never fret about their food, because they know that, however bad it may be, it would be a great deal worse to have none.

There were two gardeners once whose crops of peas had been killed by a frost. One of them fretted and grumbled, and said nobody was so unfortunate as he was. Visiting his neighbour some time after, he called out in astonishment, "What a fine crop of peas! What are these?" "These are what I sowed while you were fretting," said the other. "Why, don't you ever fret?" "Yes; but I put it off till I have repaired the mischief." "But then you have no need to fret at all." "That's very true," said the other; "and that's just the reason why I put it off."

Some children have *selfish* tempers. They always think of themselves first, and help themselves to the best of everything. A little girl belonging to this class, whose name was Mary, was out visiting once with her mother. She had a little brother called Charlie, who was left at home. The lady at whose house they were visiting gave Mary two peaches. One of them was a nice, plump, mellow, juicy peach, that would make your mouth water to look at it. The other was a poor-looking one with a great spot on the side, showing that it was half rotten. Mary began at once very eagerly to eat up the ripe peach. Presently her mother said to her, "Mary, my child, are you not going to save some for Charlie?" "Oh, yes, ma," said Mary; "I am saving *the rotten one for Charlie!*" And people who indulge this selfish feeling while they are young will find it remain with them when they grow up. There is one place in the Bible in which God complained of the Jews that they kept the best of their lambs and sheep in their flocks, and offered Him "the lame and blind." The people who would do this, when they are grown up, are the very ones who, when young, would "keep the rotten one for Charlie." And these sort of people are to be found among us as well as among the Jews. Look at that plate on which the Communion collection has just been taken up in church. See; there's a counterfeit coin. And there are two or three other pieces so plain and poor that they would not pass in business. Nobody would take them in trade. But, though not good enough to be offered in payment for meat or potatoes, somebody thought them good enough to be offered to God. I never see one of these plain coins in a collection without thinking, "Ah! that was given by one who has been accustomed from childhood 'to keep the rotten one for Charlie.'"

Other children have *generous* tempers. They always like to share what they have with others. If they have a cake, or a pie, or something very nice to eat, they do not sneak away into a corner and eat it all themselves: they love to go among their brothers and sisters or companions and share it with them. They feel happier for it, and have much more enjoyment of the part they do eat in this way than if they had eaten it all. It is said of Alfred, the great and good king of England, that, during the time in which he was driven by the Danes from his throne, and was wandering in disguise and poverty, he was reduced so low that a part of a loaf of bread was all his supply. While in this state a hungry beggar approached him and implored relief. The generous monarch opened his wallet and shared freely his last morsel with one of the humblest of his subjects. And he who could act thus as a man must have been accustomed to act so when a child. And these tempers indulged are part of the "doings" of a child by which he may be known.

But, again, *by the habits he forms*, as well as by the tempers he indulges, a child may be known. By habits we mean the ways in which we are accustomed to do things. Somebody once said that "man is a bundle of habits." And this is just as true of boys and girls as it is of men and women. Indeed, it is while we are young that we tie up this bundle. And as it is a bundle we carry with us all our lives, we should be very careful what we put into the bundle. Some children form *idle* habits. They love to lie in bed late in the morning. It is hard to waken them and get them up; and when they are up it is hard to get them to work or study, or do anything but play or loiter about. These sort of children remind one very much of the farmer's horse. This horse, the farmer said, had only two faults. One was, that he was very hard to catch. The other was, that when he was caught he wasn't good for anything. Other children have *industrious* habits. They rise early; they study hard, and get their lessons well. If they are set to work they do it cheerfully; they are not easily tired, but keep on until the work is done. People with these habits always succeed in life. There is no difficulty which industry has not conquered. One day a load of coal was thrown down before the door of a cellar in which a poor family lived. A little girl went out with quite a small shovel and began to shovel it up. "My little child," said a gentleman who was passing by, "you can't get all that coal in with your small shovel." "Oh, yes, I can, sir," said the little girl, "*if I only work long enough.*"

There was a poor boy once who resolved to get an education. He had to work hard all day, and, when evening came, he had no place to read in, and no light to read by; so he used to take his book and go into the street, and stand by some shop window and study in the light that shone from it. And sometimes, when the stores were closed before he got through, he would climb up a lamp-post and hold on with one hand while he held his book with the other. It is not surprising that he became a man who was distinguished for his learning.

Some children form *careless habits*. They never put things in their proper places, but lay them down and leave them just where they may happen to be. Then, when they want them, they can't tell where to find them. Suppose you were visiting in a family where several children live who have formed careless habits. The morning hour for going to school has come. There is a great noise and confusion in the entry. You go to your room door to find out what is the matter, and you hear sounds like these: "Where's my hat?" "Where's my bonnet?" "Who's taken my books?" "Somebody's always taking my things. I do wish people would mind their own business, and let my things alone!" Poor children! Who has been taking their things and teazing them so? Nobody at all. Their things are just where they left them; and they find them presently, one in the parlour, another in the dining-room, and another in the kitchen. Now, there is no telling, my dear children, how much evil sometimes results from the formation of careless habits. Several years ago a dreadful explosion of gunpowder took place in Wilmington, Delaware. Three large waggons were carrying powder in kegs from Mr Dupont's mills on the Brandywine to a place on the Delaware. As they were passing the outskirts of the city, and while just opposite the beautiful mansion of Bishop Lee, there was a flash—a tremendous noise— and all was over. In an instant the waggons, the horses, the drivers, and all about them were blown to atoms. Nobody ever could tell exactly how it took place. But, if the truth were known, I dare say it would be found that an act of carelessness was the cause of it. Suppose, for instance, that a cooper of careless habits had made one of the kegs. While making the keg he took up one of the staves which had a little hole in it. He was too careless to notice it, or to mind it if it was noticed. He put that stave in the keg. The keg was taken to the mill and filled with powder. The waggon is loaded. That keg is put in. The motion of the waggon shakes the powder through the hole. Presently a spark, either struck by the horse's shoe or coming from some other source, lights on the scattered grains, and the awful mischief is done. How many a calamity, equally terrible, has been caused by a single act of carelessness!

Other children form *careful habits*. They never waste anything. In regard to time, and money, and everything else, they remember our Saviour's words, "Gather up the fragments, that nothing be lost." They put things in their proper places, and always know where to find them. Their rule is: "A place for everything, and everything in its place." It is an excellent rule, and attention to it will work wonders. Those who form habits of this kind, when they grow up are almost sure to be rich and useful. Two gentlemen were once engaged in procuring subscriptions to the Bible Society. As they passed by a fine large house they heard the gentleman who lived there reproving the servants in the kitchen for extravagance in throwing away the ends of candles and half-burned lamp-lighters. "Well," said one of the collectors to the other, "it's not worth while to stop here; for a man who is so careful about the ends of his candles will hardly give anything for the Bible." "It will do no harm to try," said the other. They went in, and were agreeably surprised at receiving a very large subscription. "Sir," said one of the collectors, "the amount of your subscription greatly surprises us. For when we heard you, a few moments ago, reproving your servants for not saving the ends of candles, we thought it hardly worth while to stop." "Ah! gentlemen," said he, "it is by the habit of carefulness in little things that I am able to give largely to the Bible Society and other good causes."

A young man once went into the city of Paris to seek a situation. He had letters of recommendation to a large banking establishment. He called on the gentleman who was at the head of it, full of hope and confidence that he should find employment. The gentleman heard what he had to say, and looked over his letters hastily, and then handed them back to him, saying, "We have nothing for you to do, sir." The young man felt his heart sink within him. He was ready to burst into tears. But there was no help for it. So he made his bow and retired. But, as he was passing in front of the building, there was a pin lying on the pavement. He stopped, stooped down, and picked it up, and then stuck it carefully away under the bosom of his coat. Now, it happened so that the gentleman with whom he had just been speaking was standing at the window and saw what took place. In an instant the thought occurred to him that the young man who had such habits of carefulness as to stop in such a moment of disappointment and pick up a pin would make a useful business man. He sent immediately and called him back. He gave him an humble situation in the establishment. From that he rose by degrees till he became the principal partner in the concern, and, eventually, a man of immense wealth, and the chief banker in Paris. Here was the case of a young man who, through habits of carefulness, may be said to have *made his fortune by a pin.*

Some children form *dilatory habits.* They will do what they are told, but they never do it *right-away.* For example, Mary is a dilatory girl. If her mother says to her, " Mary, go upstairs and bring me the baby's blue frock from the closet." " Yes, ma," says Mary, " I'll go in a minute;" and then she will go on with her reading or play, and keep her mother waiting for a quarter of an hour. John is a dilatory boy. His father said to him one day, " John, I want you to take this letter to the post-office directly after dinner." " Yes, sir," said John. But after dinner he went to play for an hour or two. Then it was too late for the mail; and this was the cause of a very serious loss to his father. That boy will be one of those who are always too late. When going on a journey, he will reach the wharf two or three minutes after the boat has started. He will learn to put off doing things at the right time when he is young, and the habit will remain with him when he grows up. He will learn to do this in little things, and then he will go on to do it in great things. And in just this way multitudes will lose their souls at last. When Elizabeth, the great and gifted but ambitious queen of England, was dying, she cried out, " An inch of time. Millions of money for an inch of time!" Poor woman! she was lying on a splendid bed; she had been used to have a new dress every day; she had ten thousand dresses in her wardrobe, and at her feet a kingdom on which the sun never sets; but all was of no value then. She had lived for seventy years, but had put off preparation for eternity to the last. That which should have occupied her whole lifetime was crowded into a few moments; and, when it was too late, the wealth of her kingdom would have been given for "an inch of time!"

Other children form *prompt habits*. When they are told to do anything, they go and do it at once. If they are reading when called, they will lay the book down in a moment. If they are at play, they break off without any delay, and hasten to do what is required of them. And this habit is of great importance in order to success in life. General Washington was never known to fail in meeting an engagement, or even to be late at an engagement, in all his life. This is a most valuable habit to form, and one which every person should acquire who desires to succeed in life.

And then the *company which he keeps* goes far to make up those "doings" of a child by which he may be known. The choice of companions is a very important thing. Few things have more to do with the formation of our character than the company we keep. You can generally tell what sort of a person any one is by noticing what kind of company he chooses.

Now, the other question is: *What may be known of a child by his doings?* This can be answered in much shorter time than the other. And, in answering it, we may say that you can tell a child's *fortune* by his doings. There are some wicked persons who pretend to be fortune-tellers, and to be able to find out in various ways all about what will happen to anybody for years to come. And many people are foolish enough to believe them. These people mean, by *fortune*, the things which they suppose will happen to them as if it were by chance. But there is no such thing as fortune in *this* sense. Our word "fortune" comes from the name of one of the idol-gods that used to be worshipped by the Romans. They called this god Fortuna. She was represented as a female blindfolded, and having a horn of plenty in one hand, out of which she scattered blessings among the people at haphazard, without any knowledge or discrimination. Now, we all know, my dear children, that this is a heathen idea. There is no such person or thing as fortune in this sense. And it is just as well to avoid the use of the word, or at least to avoid attaching any such idea to it. The blessings we receive are not given to us by blind chance. The Bible tells us that "every good gift, and every perfect gift, is from above, and cometh down from the Father of lights." Again it tells us that it is God who gives us "life, and breath, and *all* things." But God does not shut His eyes, neither is He blindfolded, when He bestows blessings on His people. No; He does it with His eyes open. He knows what He gives, and He knows to whom He gives it. And He gives the best things He has to those who love Him most. I do not mean by this that He gives the most money, or the largest proportion of the good things of this life, to those who love Him. Oh, no; for these are not by any means the best things God has to give. His grace, and His spirit, and the things which belong to salvation—*these* are God's best gifts. These are His real good things. And these He has promised to give to those who love Him.

But you may ask, What has all this to do with telling a child's fortune? And how can this be told by his doings? Why, it has a good deal to do with it; and let me show you how. God has commanded us to do certain things. If we do them, He has promised to bless us and make us happy. It is only the blessing of God that will give us a good fortune. If we fail to obtain His blessing we shall have a bad fortune. And if you want to find out whether any person is likely to receive God's blessing, you must inquire whether he is doing what God commands him to

THE INDUSTRIOUS FARMER.—*Rills from the Fountain of Life*, p. 121.

HOW FORTUNES MAY BE TOLD.

do. And how can we tell this? Why, by looking at "his doings." God's commands to us refer to our "doings." That is, they refer to "the tempers we indulge, and the habits we form, and the company we keep."

Now, show me a child who is cross, and fretful, and selfish in his temper; who is idle, and careless, and dilatory in his habits; and who keeps company with persons like himself or worse; and I will tell you that child's fortune just as easily as I could tell you how many twice five make in addition. That child will grow up to be poor, and miserable, and good for nothing in this world; and in the world to come he will be unhappy for ever. But show me a child who is striving, by the help of God, to be kind, and patient, and generous in his temper; industrious, and careful, and prompt in his habits; and who keeps company with those who love and fear God, and is striving to become like them; and I will tell you that child's fortune just as easily as in the other case.

You can tell what the farmer's fortune will be when you see him rising early and working late, and ploughing, and sowing, and tilling his grounds with untiring care and industry. You can tell what the merchant's fortune will be when you see him always in his place, and doing everything in his power to make his business prosper. Solomon says, "Seest thou a man diligent in his business? he shall stand before kings." That means, he will be sure to succeed.

Bear in mind, my dear children, that you are making your fortunes now every day. You have read in storybooks about persons "going off to *seek* their fortunes." You can do this just as well by staying at home, and a great deal better too. You are all busy now in making your fortunes. The tempers you are indulging, the habits you are forming, and the company you are keeping, are all helping to make them. What kind of tempers, and habits, and company are they? What an important question this is! How careful you should be to find out what is wrong in your tempers or habits, and pray to God to help you to correct it at once! It is very easy to do it now. It will be very hard by-and-by.

If you wish to succeed, you must pray for Jesus to help you. Without Him we can do nothing. But by His help we can do all things. And if we have His grace given to us, then we shall be able to have our ways ordered so as to please Him; we shall "love the things which He commands, and desire those which He does promise; and so, among the sundry and manifold changes of the world, our hearts will surely then be fixed where true joys are to be found." And the Lord grant that this may be the case with us all, for Jesus' sake! Amen.

THE MILLENNIAL MENAGERIE.

" The wolf also shall dwell with the lamb, and the leopard shall lie down with the kid; and the calf and the young lion and the fatling together; and a little child shall lead them."—ISAIAH, xi. 6.

I REMEMBER, several years ago, my dear children, when returning from England in a packet-ship, there was a little boy among the steerage passengers who became a great favourite with those on board. He was not more than three or four years old. And, as he had been so unfortunate as to lose the use of one eye, but had a good voice, and was very fond of singing, which he did very well, the cabin passengers all took a great interest in him. Very often, after dinner, we would call him upon the quarter-deck and bribe him to sing for us by offering him nuts and raisins. Among the pieces that he liked most to sing, and that we were the most fond of hearing, was one about " The good time coming." When a circle of listeners was gathered round him, and the tempting reward of his performances had been exhibited to him, he would clear his throat and turn up the white of his blind eye very funnily, and begin:—

> " There's a good time coming;
> There's a good time coming;
> Boys, wait a little longer.
> We may not live to see the day,
> But earth shall glitter in the ray
> Of the good time coming."

I suppose this poor child did not understand the real meaning of the words he used to sing. He never thought, perhaps, that he was singing about a time of which God has spoken in the Bible, and the coming of which is just as certain as it is that the sun will set to-night and rise again to-morrow morning. This time is commonly called the millennium. This name is not given to it in the Bible. Millennium means a thousand years. And, as the Bible tells us that this "good time coming" will last a thousand years, that is the reason why this name has been given to it.

The prophet Isaiah was speaking of this time when he wrote the words of our text. When it comes Satan will not be permitted to go about the earth and tempt people as he does now; but he will be driven out and fastened up in the bottomless pit, and made to stay there all the time. There will be no sickness in the world then; no sorrow, and no sin. No earthquakes will rend the ground; no storms nor tempests will sweep over it. No scorching heat nor biting frosts will be experienced then. No wars will then be waged; no blood will then be shed; no violence nor quarrelling will then be heard. All the people in the earth will then be good and holy. There will be as much beauty and happiness all over the world then as there was in the garden of Eden before Adam sinned. Earth will then be like heaven. All the people of the world will then be under one government. The capital of that government will be Jerusalem, which will be rebuilt in great glory. And Jesus will be the head of that government. He will not be on the earth all the time, but He will occupy the throne of David at Jerusalem, and will often appear in great glory to His people there.

Many wonderful sights will be witnessed when this time comes. One of these will be that which the prophet Isaiah describes in our text. You have often been to the menagerie to see a collection of wild animals. But you have always seen them put in separate cages, with strong iron bars, to keep them from devouring one another, or from tearing to pieces the people who came near them. But here the prophet describes to us a millennial menagerie. They will need no separate cages nor iron bars then. For then "the wolf shall dwell with the lamb, and the leopard shall lie down with the kid; and the calf and the young lion and the fatling together; and a little child shall lead them." And in the next verses the prophet goes on to say, "And the cow and the bear shall feed; their young ones shall lie down together: and the lion shall eat straw like the ox. And the sucking child shall play on the hole of the asp, and the weaned child shall put his hand on the cockatrice's den. They shall not hurt nor destroy in all My holy mountain: for the earth shall be full of the knowledge of the Lord, as the waters cover the sea."

Now, we may consider the prophet in our text as teaching us two important things.

In the first place, he points out to us here the change which will take place in the wild beasts to fit them for the millennium.

And, in the second place, he points out the change which must take place in us to fit us for heaven.

"The wolf shall dwell with the lamb, and the leopard shall lie down with the kid; and the calf and the young lion and the fatling together; and a little child shall lead them." This shows us the change that will take place in the wild beasts to fit them for the millennium. From what is here said we learn that they will lose their fierceness and all their savage qualities. They will no longer fight, and tear, and devour each other. Now, we are accustomed from our childhood to repeat and sing the words of Dr Watts's sweet and simple hymn,—

> "Let dogs delight to bark and bite,
> For God has made them so;
> Let bears and lions growl and fight,
> For 'tis their nature too."

But this hymn will have to be altered when the millennium comes. Then the dogs will no longer delight to bark and bite. Then it will not be the nature of the bears and lions to growl and fight. It would be a slander upon the animals to sing this hymn about them then. They will not live upon one another then, but upon grass and vegetables. Then, the prophet says, "the lion will eat straw like the ox." Now, some good people always smile when they hear anybody say this. They point to the teeth of the lion or the bear, or to their stomachs, and say, "Why, don't you see that these are not adapted to eat or digest anything but animal food? It is impossible that these animals should ever live on grass or vegetables." Well, then, you are ready to ask, "What do these people do with the words of our text and similar passages in the Bible?" I'll tell you what they do with them. They say that these words are only figurative, and that the wild beasts here spoken of mean wicked men; and that the change in the habits of the beasts refers to the change that will take place then in the tempers and dispositions of men. But this is not the meaning of these passages, my dear children. They mean *just what they say*. The prophets were not using figures, but stating facts, when they uttered these words. The wild beasts of the earth, as well as the men, and women, and children living in it, will share in the blessedness of the millennium when it comes; and *their* share of that blessedness will lie in just the change spoken of in the text. And I wish now to give you three good and sufficient reasons for the view I am taking. *The first reason is, that the state of the world then will make this change in the animals necessary.* The world itself will be different from what it is now. Its climate and seasons will be different: its vegetable productions will be different; "instead of the thorn shall come up the fir-tree; instead of the brier, the myrtle-tree; the wilderness and the solitary place shall be glad, and the desert shall rejoice and blossom as the rose." Its inhabitants will be different; "the people shall be all righteous, and they shall know the Lord, from the least even unto the greatest of them." And when everything else is changed, is it likely that there will be no change in the animals? Surely not. To change everything else

GOD ABLE TO CHANGE ANIMALS.

and leave the animals unchanged would spoil the beauty and harmony of the scene.

Another reason for believing that this will be so is that God is able to do it. Nobody will deny this. He can easily do whatever He wants to do. Nothing is impossible with God. And not only is nothing impossible, but nothing is difficult or hard for Him to do. God can make a world as easily as He can make a grain of sand. God can change the teeth and stomachs of wild beasts just as easily as He can change the hearts and tempers of wicked men. But everybody allows that wicked men will be changed when the millennium comes. They allow that God's power is able to make *this* change. But should they not allow that the wild beasts will be changed also? Is not the same power which makes one of these changes just as able to make the other also? And has not God promised, just as plainly and positively, to do one of these things as He has to do the other? This, then, is a good reason why we should expect to see it done.

And then there is *a third reason* why this change in the animals should take place, and that is, that *it will only be restoring them to the condition in which they were created in the beginning*. God did not make the beasts of the earth *wild* at the first. The animals did not devour one another or live on flesh when they were in the garden of Eden. Grass was their food then; and why may it not be so again? God said expressly to Adam (see Gen. i. 30), "To *every beast of the earth*, and to every fowl of the air, and to everything that creepeth upon the earth, wherein there is life, *I have given every green herb for meat.*" God made the animals live on vegetables then, just as man did. And it was very probable that they had nothing else to eat till after the deluge. We know very well that God never gave men permission to eat flesh till after Noah came out of the ark. And it is most likely that He did the same with the beasts. And since we know that the millennium—the "good time coming"—

is intended to put the world itself, and the people who live in it, back in the position which they occupied before Adam sinned, why should it not put the animals back into the same state also? I think, my dear children, that these reasons are sufficient to show that the words of our text mean just what they say; then when lions, and bears, and wolves are spoken of, it is not men and women who are intended, but real live lions, and bears, and wolves; and that when a change in their dispositions and habits is spoken of, it means a real change in these animals themselves—such a change as will be necessary to fit them for the state of things that will exist in the millennium. This is the first thing which the prophet teaches us in the text. What a pleasant thing it will be when this comes to pass! Then there will be no insects to sting; no serpents to bite; and no wild beasts to devour. Young children in the millennium will be able to make pets and playthings of little lions, and tigers, and bears, and wolves, just as they do now of rabbits, and squirrels, and guinea-pigs. And I suppose that when Isaiah wrote the words of our text he meant to give us a pictorial view of the way in which a millennial boy would gather a menagerie of animals around him for his amusement, and lead them through the woods, or play with them on the lawn before his father's house, just as we have sometimes seen boys playing in our times with a lamb, or a kid, or a dog. A fine time for play the boys and girls will have in those days!

But there is another thing which we may consider this text as teaching us; and *that is the change which must take place in us in order that we may be fit for heaven.*

Now, I have said, my dear children, that the animals spoken of in our text do not mean human beings—men, women, and children; and that is very true. Our text in its true meaning refers to real animals, and nothing else. But the Bible does sometimes represent different sorts of people under the figure of different animals. For instance, you remember, in one of His parables in which Jesus was

THE WOLF CLASS.

speaking of the day of judgment, He compared the good people, on His right hand, to sheep; and the wicked, on His left, to goats. In another place He compares false teachers to ravening wolves. And in the twenty-second Psalm the wicked men who crucified Jesus are spoken of as dogs, as strong bulls, as unicorns, and roaring lions. And so, although this is not what the prophet means, we may consider the different animals here spoken of as representing different kinds of children, and thus we may look upon this passage as pointing out the change which they must experience if they hope to enter heaven.

Let us see, now, how many of these wild animals are spoken of in our text. There is the wolf, and the leopard, and the lion, and, in the verse following, the bear. These may be regarded as representing four classes of children whose characters correspond to the qualities which mark these different animals, and who must all be changed in order to make them fit for heaven.

Now, the first class of characters represented here is the WOLF *class.* This is a large class. It takes in all who may be described as *cross* children. This is the quality which we most commonly associate with the thought of the wolf. He is cross, snappish, and quarrelsome. He is all the time growling and showing his teeth. He seems to be continually on the watch for a cause of quarrel with somebody; and if he cannot *find* a cause he will *make* one. We see this quality exhibited in the fable of the wolf and the lamb who met at the same stream of water to get a drink. The wolf was at the upper part of the stream, and the lamb at the lower part. The wolf looked angrily at the lamb, and asked him how he dared to come and muddle the water while he was drinking? The poor lamb very meekly replied by observing that he was the lower down the stream of the two, and, therefore, if he made any disturbance in the water, it would flow down the stream and not up it. Upon this the wolf flew into a passion, and charged the lamb with contradicting him, and presuming to know more than he did; and then he sprang upon the lamb and tore him in pieces. This was acting out the wolf's character completely. And this is very much the spirit which cross children manifest. You can scarcely speak to them or look at them but they have something sharp and unkind to say. All such children belong to the *wolf* class. And they must be changed before they can be fit to enter heaven. Jesus is called "the Lamb of God;" and if cross children who are like wolves hope to dwell with Him, all their crossness must be overcome. They must become gentle, and kind, and lamb-like, as Jesus is. And then, when they are happy with Him in heaven, it may well be said that the wolf is dwelling with the lamb.

The second class of character here described is the LEOPARD *class.* The quality which marks the leopard or the tiger (for they are nearly alike) is *cruelty*. This is stamped upon his countenance. You can see it glaring out in the fierceness of his eye. Every look that you take at him suggests the idea of cruelty. And all the habits of the leopard show that this is really his character. There is nothing kind or generous about him. The lion will only kill in self-defence or to satisfy his hunger. But the leopard will kill for the mere love of killing. Cruelty is a part of his nature, and he delights to indulge it. One lamb or sheep is as much as he can eat at a meal; and yet he will worry and kill a whole flock to gratify his cruelty and indulge his fondness for shedding blood.

This class of children, I am glad to say, is much smaller than the first that we spoke of; but yet a good many belong to it. You can tell a leopard **as** soon as you see him by his spots. And there are certain things about the children of this class which may be looked upon as the spots which prove that they belong to the leopard tribe.

When you see children worrying and distressing poor helpless creatures who are in their power; when you see them catching flies and killing them, or pulling off their wings and watching them hop about in their misery; when you see them beating or unkindly treating some poor little kitten or dog that they are playing with; when you see a set of boys pelting the frogs beside the brook or pond, or throwing stones at the old lame horse as he limps over the commons trying to pick up a little grass, or teasing the old blind beggar as he gropes his tottering way from door to door, seeking relief in his poverty; or when you see the larger boys and girls in a family uniting in some trick to frighten a younger brother or sister, and then laughing heartily when the cries and shrieks of the little terrified one are heard,—oh, *this* is cruel indeed!— then, my dear children, you may point to these things and say, "There, there are the leopard spots." You may know in a moment to what class these children belong.

But there is no cruelty in heaven; and none with cruel dispositions can enter there. Heaven is a place where love and kindness prevail. God is love: and Jesus is love. Love is, as it were, the atmosphere which all breathe in heaven. And wherever there is a child whose disposition is marked by unkindness and cruelty, he belongs to the leopard class: he must be changed if he hopes to go to heaven.

The third kind of character here described is the LION *class.* "The calf and the *young lion* and the fatling together." The lion is always called the "king of beasts." He has some very fine and generous qualities. These, of course, will not require to be changed. It is not these that are referred to here. Only that which is wrong will need to be altered; and only this, therefore, in each of the animals can be intended. And the quality in the lion that I suppose we are chiefly to look at is his *pride*. It seems as if he knew that he was regarded as the head of all the animals. How stately is his walk! How high he carries his head! How he seems to look down on all the inhabitants of the forest, as though none of them were good enough to range over the same fields or dwell in the same woods with him! A look of proud disdain may be seen in every glance of his eye and in every motion of his noble form.

Now, this class of children is very large. How many here are under the influence of *pride* in different ways! You may see pride in the toss of a child's head, in the glance of his eye, in the curl of his lip, and in the haughtiness of manner which seems to say to those about him, especially if they happen to be poorer than himself, "Stand off; you are not good enough to keep company with me." My dear children, of all the feelings that people indulge, pride is the most unmeaning, the most ridiculous, and among the most sinful. Some one has said that "pride was not made for man." This is very true. Nobody in the world, not even the richest or wisest or greatest or best man that lives, has anything to feel proud of, and no right to feel proud at all. There is no pride in heaven. There were some angels there once who began to feel proud. But God drove them out immediately, and would not let them stay there. And no people who indulge proud feelings will be allowed to enter heaven. Jesus says, "Learn of me, for I am meek and *lowly*." If we have proud hearts, they must be changed before we can hope to go to heaven.

But there is a fourth kind of character represented in this menagerie, and that is the BEAR *class.* In the verse just after the text it says, "The cow and the *bear* shall feed." There is no difficulty at all in telling the quality which distinguishes the bear. He is known all over the world for his *sullenness*. Nothing is more common than to say of a rude, disagreeable person that he is "as surly as a bear." No matter how kindly you may treat a bear, or how many good things you may give him, it seems to make no impression upon him. He never does anything to testify his gratitude. If you speak kindly to a dog, and throw him a crust of bread or a bone, he will wag his tail and caper about, and try as plainly as he can to say, "Thank you, thank you; I'm very much obliged to you." But you would have to give a great many crusts of bread to a bear before you would get a wag of his tail or anything expressive of his gratitude. He remains the same sullen, surly, sulky beast all the time.

Now, the children in this class, I am thankful to say, are not so numerous as in some of the others. But there are a good many who act the bear's part very well. They look all the time sour and displeased. They seldom have anything to say, and when they do make out to speak it is generally something so rough and rude that they had much better have left it unsaid. They hardly ever look pleasant or act kindly. And if they are spoken to they generally growl out a "yes," or "no," or the shortest and surliest possible reply. But when the bear comes to feed with the cow in the millennium, he will be a very different kind of animal from what he is now. And if the children of the *bear class* wish to know what they must become like in order to make them fit for heaven, they can easily find out by reading and meditating on such passages as these:—"As ye would that men should do to you, even so do to them." "Be pitiful; be *courteous.*" "Put on, therefore, as the elect of God, bowels of mercies, kindness, humbleness of mind, meekness, longsuffering; forbearing one another and forgiving one another, even as Christ forgave you." "Let all bitterness and wrath and anger be put away from you, with all malice. And *be ye kind* one to another, tender-hearted, forgiving one another, even as God, for Christ's sake, hath forgiven you." When these surly children learn to exercise the sweet spirit described in these passages, there will be a greater change wrought in them than that which the bear will exhibit when he learns to feed in the meadow with the cow.

These four are all the animals spoken of in this millennial menagerie. But I wish to add two others to them in order to make the collection more complete.

We may speak of a fifth description of character which it would be well to consider, and that is the MULE *class.* We all know what the character of the mule is. The thing which has always distinguished him is his *obstinacy* or *stubbornness*. When he takes a notion he's fixed in it. You can't whip him out of it; you can't coax him out of it. The more you want him to do anything he doesn't like, the more he won't. The rule of his conduct seems to be just this,—

> "If I will, *I will*, you may depend on't;
> But if I won't, I won't, and there's an end on't."

This is the mule all over. And how many children are just like this! Asking, reasoning, coaxing, threatening, are all lost on them. They are so hard to bend that they put you in mind of live crowbars. They are so obstinate and mule-like that you almost feel tempted to measure their ears and see if there is not some sign of relationship to that long-eared animal. My dear children, who belong to this class, you must be changed and get rid of this obstinacy if you hope to enter heaven. And if you wish to know just the lesson you must learn, just the feature in those fit for heaven which you should try most to imitate, you will find it in James, iii. 17. It is this:—"*Easy to be entreated.*" Think of this when the next obstinate fit comes on, and pray God to make you "easy to be entreated."

The sixth and last description of character that I would refer to is included in the FOX *class.* The thing which characterises the fox is his *cunning*. He is a low, mean, cringing animal, full of tricks and falsehood. He is not ashamed to rob or steal if he can only avoid being caught. And the fox class of children, I am sorry to say, is not small. They all have a *sly* way of doing wrong things. They seem to have no sense of the difference between right and wrong in certain things. But they have a very keen sense of the difference between being found out and *not* being found out. They are always ready to slip into the pantry and take a little sugar or preserves, or some of the cakes put away there, if they think they can only do it unobserved, as the fox creeps into the hen-roost when the farmer is away or the dog is asleep.

But the fox will have to quit his mean cunning tricks

and take to some honest way of getting a living when the millennium comes. And so all the children of this class must be changed and give up their trickery and cunning if they would be made fit for heaven. There will be no liars in heaven. None who use deceit and guile can enter there. Honesty, sincerity, plain-dealing, and straightforwardness must be the character of those who desire to share the joys of that blessed place. You must either give up the thought of going to heaven, or else you must give up all deceit and cunning.

Now, my dear children, I want you to ask yourselves, individually, "To which of these classes do I belong? Is it the wolf, or the leopard, or the lion, or the bear, or the mule, or the fox that represents my character? Am I cross? or cruel? or proud? or surly? or stubborn? or sly?" And, when you find out what your fault is, pray God to give you grace to overcome it. If you want to stop the leak in a vessel, you must first find out where it is. If you wish to extinguish a fire, you must ascertain what is burning. And so it is here. You must know just what your fault is, and then try to get it changed.

We have been talking about the millennium. The question is, What can we do to help it on? We can do *two* things. *We can try to get our own hearts changed.* This will help it on. It will not come till all the people that God has given to Jesus to be His children are brought to know, and love, and serve Him. While our hearts are unchanged we are hindrances in the way of its coming. When our hearts are changed, that very change will help on the millennium.

And then we can help to send the Gospel to others who are without it. This, too, will hasten its coming. Jesus said, "The Gospel must be preached *for a witness* to all nations, and then it will come." We do not have to wait till all nations are converted, but only till they have had opportunity of hearing the Gospel, and then the millennium will come. So that when we send the Bible to the heathen, or send the missionary to preach it to them, we are doing the very things that God would have us do in order to hasten the time when "the wolf shall dwell with the lamb, and the leopard shall lie down with the kid; and the calf and the young lion and the fatling together; and a little child shall lead them." Then let us seek to get our own evil natures changed, and let us do all we can to send the Gospel to those who are without it. And, as we do this, let our constant prayer be, "Thy kingdom come!" or, in the beautiful lines of Bishop Heber's missionary hymn,—

> "Waft, waft, ye winds, His story,
> And you, ye waters, roll,
> Till, like a sea of glory,
> It spreads from pole to pole;
> Till o'er our ransomed nature
> The Lamb for sinners slain—
> Redeemer, King, Creator—
> In bliss returns to reign."

THE BEST MERCHANDISE.

" The merchandise of it is better than the merchandise of silver."—
Prov. iii. 14.

A merchant is one who buys and sells. Merchandise denotes the *things* which a merchant buys and sells. If you walk along Market Street you will find merchants there of different kinds. Some of them are dry-goods merchants, some of them are hardware merchants, some of them are china merchants; and you will see their merchandise in the boxes or bales lying along the street.

But the merchandise spoken of in our text is very different from this. Here Solomon says, "the merchandise of *it.*" Now, the question is, What does this *it* refer to? The merchandise of what? If you look back to the verse before our text you will find that Solomon is saying there, "Happy is the man that findeth *wisdom;*" and then he goes on to say in our text, "for the merchandise of it is better than the merchandise of silver."

The "it," then, refers to wisdom; and wisdom, you know, my dear children, means *true religion*—the love and fear of God. There is a text in the Proverbs which says, "The fear of the Lord is the beginning of wisdom." This shows us what wisdom means.

Now, we learn from this text, then, that to deal in wisdom—to be concerned with religion—is better than to deal in anything else. "The merchandise of wisdom is better than the merchandise of silver."

If you had a mine of gold or of silver on your farm,

and you were occupied in getting out the gold or silver and selling it, then this gold and silver would be your merchandise; these would be the things with which you were trading. And if you had such mines upon your farm, you would not be willing to work as a bricklayer or shoemaker, because you would have your merchandise in gold and silver, and you would think it better to be occupied with these things than with anything else. But here we learn from Solomon that the merchandise of wisdom is *better* than even that of silver or gold.

And now the question comes up, *Why* is the merchandise of wisdom better than that of silver?

I wish to point out several reasons why it is so—why this is the *best* merchandise that any person can engage in.

The *first* reason is: *Because it is a business you can begin sooner than you can any other.*

If you wish to be a lawyer, or a physician, or a minister, you must finish your education, and go through a long course of study to fit you for the important duties you will have to perform. You must wait till you are twenty-one years of age before you can begin to enter these professions. So if you wish to be a carpenter, or a printer, or a dry-goods merchant, you must serve an apprenticeship to these different sorts of business, and wait till you get to be of age before you can set up for yourselves.

But it is very different with the merchandise of which we are now speaking. You can begin this to-day. The youngest among you can begin it without waiting another hour. Why, children as young as four and five years old have begun to be wisdom's merchants, and have found the merchandise of it better than the merchandise of silver!

We read in the Bible of "little Samuel," who was called to be wisdom's merchant when he was quite young. I suppose he was not more than seven or eight years of age when God first called him, and when he began to trade in wisdom. Then we read of Timothy, who, " from a child, had known the Scriptures, which were able to make him wise unto salvation."

Did you ever think how much God has done to show His interest in children and His earnest desire to have them engaged in the merchandise of wisdom? Why, if He had done nothing more than to write in His blessed Word that one sweet promise which we find in Prov. viii. 17—" Those that seek Me *early* shall find Me "—it ought to encourage every child who reads the Bible to begin at once to serve God.

But, ah! how much more than this God has done! When He made a covenant with Abraham, and promised to be a God to him and do everything for him that was necessary for his salvation, He made Abraham bring all his children with him into fellowship with God. And He commanded the Jews, as soon as their children were eight days old, to bring them and consecrate them to Him, and cause them, as it were, with their unconscious tiny hands, to take hold of that covenant and begin to trade in wisdom's merchandise. And though baptism, the sign or seal of God's covenant as used by us, is very different from that appointed for the Jews, yet the Church of Jesus Christ is still open for children, and in their very earliest age they can be made to share in the blessings of God's covenant.

And when Jesus was on earth you know what an interest He manifested in children. Oh, how thankful every child and young person should be for what Jesus did to show His interest in them! Ah! my dear children, the sweet and gracious words of Jesus ought to engage a warm place for Him in your hearts. Jesus was fond of children; and He showed this when He rebuked His disciples for trying to send them away, and said, " Suffer the little children to come unto Me, and forbid them not; for of such is the kingdom of heaven." And then " He took them up in His arms, and put His hands upon them, and blessed them."

What blessed words these are to come from the lips of

Him who created the mighty universe, and who sits now at the right hand of the throne of God! What a surprising thing it is to know that Jesus thinks about children and loves them!—that He has made room for them in His church on earth, and room for them in His kingdom in heaven!

There is another passage in the New Testament which shows the great interest Jesus feels in children, and how anxious He is that they should be taught how to trade in "the merchandise of wisdom." One day, after His resurrection, when He was talking with Peter, who had denied Him, He asked Peter if he loved Him. Peter said to Him, very earnestly, "Yea, Lord, Thou knowest that I love Thee." And then Jesus told him what He wanted him to do, in order to show his love to Him. And what was it? It was this: "*Feed My lambs.*" Children who are trying to love and serve Jesus are His lambs. The word *to feed* in the Bible means to teach or instruct. And, when Jesus spoke these words to Peter, He meant them for all His ministers to the end of the world. It was just as if Jesus had said to every minister of the Gospel, "If you want to show your love to Me, be kind to the children in your church. Take an interest in them. Do all you can to lead them to think of Me, and to love and serve Me." It was thinking about these words of Jesus which first led me to have church once a month for children, and preach especially for them. And if ministers would only think more about these words, I feel sure they would feel more interest in their Sunday schools, and show their love to Jesus by trying to do more to feed His lambs.

And all these things show you, my dear children, that God loves to have young people serve Him; and that, although you cannot engage for yourselves in other business until you are of age, yet you are all, even the very youngest of you, old enough to engage in the merchandise of wisdom. And this is one reason why it is better than any other merchandise, because you can engage in it so much sooner.

THE SECOND REASON—EASIER.

But another reason why this merchandise is better than any other is, that *it is easier* to trade in. I mean by this that it requires less money and less labour to carry it on.

When a person is going to set up in business, the first thing that he wants is *money*. If you want to open a shop, for instance, you must have money to furnish it with the merchandise you are going to trade in. If you want to set up as a carpenter, or as a machinist, or any other trade, you must have money to furnish yourself with a shop, to provide yourself with tools, and with all the things necessary for you to carry on that trade. You can do nothing at all until you get these.

But, my dear children, no money is needed to begin to trade in the merchandise of which we are now speaking. Every one of us has all the materials ready on hand that are needed to begin this business. These materials are our sins, our evil hearts, our sinful dispositions. We are to "set up" with these, to begin with these. We are to carry these to Jesus and tell Him of them, and pray of Him the grace that will enable us to get rid of them.

This is the way in which we must begin the merchandise of wisdom. It requires no money here. When God invites people to come and buy the blessings of His grace, He says they can buy them "without money and without price."

But then, besides money, a great deal of *labour* is needed in order to be successful in any other pursuit. No farmer will succeed in the cultivation of his ground, no carpenter or tradesman will succeed in the carrying on of his design, unless he bestows upon it a great amount of labour and toil.

If you get up early in the morning, the first sounds you hear are the sounds of men hastening to their work. You find some rising as early as four o'clock, and not returning home from their labours until nine or ten o'clock at night. And we find them doing this all the time—day after day, week after week, month after month, and year after year; and all in order that they may succeed in their business.

Now, it is very hard to be doing this all the time. But God does not require such hard service on the part of those who try to love and fear Him.

I would not have you suppose, my dear children, that you can get to heaven without great efforts. It is not sitting down, and wishing yourselves in heaven that will bring you there. We are told to "*work* out our own salvation." Jesus said, "*Strive* to enter in at the strait gate." The life of the Christian is compared to a race, a struggle, a conflict. And all this implies that vigorous efforts must be put forth if we would gain the prize of eternal life. What I mean to say is, that it is easier to serve God than it is to serve Satan; that less real labour is required to secure the true riches—"the durable riches" —of the kingdom of heaven than is put forth by many to obtain the riches of this world.

Jesus said when upon earth, "Take My yoke upon you, and learn of Me; for My yoke is *easy*, and My burden is *light*." It is because Jesus makes His people love His yoke that it feels so easy, and because of the help He gives them in bearing it that His burden seems so light.

Oh, dear children, how many people there are who labour more—spend more time and pains—to secure to themselves a house of brick, or wood, or stone, that will soon crumble to decay and perish, than they are willing to put forth in order to obtain a "house not made with hands, eternal in the heavens!" How many spend more time to secure "gold that perisheth" than is needed to obtain that gold which endureth for ever and for ever!

Thus, my dear children, you see that the merchandise of wisdom is better than the merchandise of silver, because it is easier to carry it on.

But there is a *third* reason why this merchandise is better than any other; and that is, *you can have better partners here than in other pursuits.*

In carrying on important branches of business men generally have partners to engage with them. Sometimes they will have one, sometimes more. Sometimes one of the persons will bring to the concern a knowledge of the business, and another will bring the money necessary to carry it on; and then these join together to conduct the business in which they are about to engage.

But entering into partnerships is often found to be a very dangerous thing, because it is very difficult to get *good* partners.

Sometimes men find themselves connected with *dishonest* partners, who cheat them of their lawful, proper gains, and ruin the business. Sometimes they find themselves engaged with *ignorant* partners, who do not know how to carry on the business; and thus, from their want of knowledge, disaster, loss, and ruin are brought upon them.

Sometimes, too, they find themselves joined with *idle*, *careless* partners, who are unwilling to work or apply themselves as the interests of the business require; and in this way disgrace and disappointment will soon be experienced. It is often a very difficult thing to get *good* partners when they are needed.

If a young lawyer just starting in his profession could have secured Henry Clay or Daniel Webster to be his partner, how fortunate he would have thought himself! But when we begin the business of engaging in wisdom's merchandise, we have the very best partners that can be. God the Father, and God the Son, and God the Holy Ghost become the partners and helpers of all who really and earnestly engage in this business.

We have the benefit of all God's wisdom, the help of all His power, the use of all His riches, in carrying on this business. Those who become interested in it are called in the Scriptures the "heirs of God," and the "joint heirs of Jesus Christ." St Paul says of them, "They are labourers together with God." This is the same as saying that God and His people are partners. And in another place, where he is urging them to "work out their own salvation," the reason which he gives for it is that it is "God who *worketh in* them." And in one place in the

Old Testament, where God is encouraging His people to persevere in trying to get to heaven, He says, "Fear not, for *I* will *help* thee." What a blessed thing it is to have such a helper! The hardest things become easy when we have a good helper. When you have been carrying a heavy burden, and some strong person has come along and taken hold of it with you, how light it seemed! When you have had a hard lesson to learn, and some one who knew all about it has just taken a seat by your side and explained it all to you, how easy it was to learn it! Just so God helps His people to bear the burdens and learn the lessons necessary in carrying on the merchandise of wisdom.

And then the angels in heaven and all God's people on earth are the partners and helpers of those who engage in this business.

Then, my dear children, there is a *fourth* reason why this is the best merchandise to engage in: that is, *because it yields more profit than any other.*

What do men engage in business for? It is for profit, for gain. When you look out upon our streets at noonday, all crowded with men running to and fro on various errands to accomplish various ends, the great aim and object they have in view is profit or gain of some kind; they all have an eye to this. The bricklayer and the blacksmith, the carpenter, the shopkeeper, the merchant, and the salesman, are all expecting gain and profit as the result of all their labour. And it is right to look for it, and right that they should have it.

But, my dear children, should we try to make money by religion? Should we engage in the merchandise of wisdom for the purpose of getting gain of this kind from it? No; not at all.

And yet, see what our text says:—"The merchandise of it is *better* than the merchandise of silver." Does the Bible teach us that it is profitable to serve God? Yes; it certainly does. It says that in keeping the commandments of the Lord there is "*great reward.*" It tells us that "godliness is profitable unto all things; having promise of the life that now is and of that which is to come." It yields a greater profit and a better gain than gold or silver.

And do you ask me what this gain is? I answer, it will secure the pardon of sin; it will secure to you peace and happiness here, and a treasure in the heavens that will last for ever hereafter.

We read in the Bible of the rich man and Lazarus. We are not told how this man made his money. He had probably been a merchant, and made it in the buying and selling of merchandise. He had retired from business, and was living at his ease upon the great gains he had secured for himself. But while attending to these things he had forgotten the concerns of his soul; he had laid up no riches for the world to come.

There was a poor beggar who was laid at his gate, and asked only for the crumbs which fell from the rich man's table.

But, oh, what a wonderful change took place in the condition of these two men when they died! The rich man on earth became the poor man after death; and the poor beggar on earth became the rich man in heaven. The reason was, my dear children, that while he had engaged in no earthly business, he had not forgotten the merchandise of wisdom; and he found, to his everlasting happiness, that "the merchandise of it is better than the merchandise of silver."

There is one other reason why this is the best of all merchandise; and that is, that *there is more room for engaging in it than in any other.*

Can you think of any one kind of business in which all that are here present could engage at once? Could you all become ministers, or all lawyers, or all physicians, or all dry-goods merchants, or all storekeepers, or all carpenters? Certainly not. Some of you would not be fit for one of these professions, or trades, or employments, and some would not be fit for others.

And even if you were all fit for any one of them, there would not be room for you all to enter upon it at once. You would not be wanted. You could not find employment. It would be impossible for you to succeed.

But how different it is with the business of serving God! Here there is room enough for you all. It is a merchandise which all can understand; a pursuit for which all are fit. Just look for a moment at some of the things which those must have who engage in this business, and then you will see who are fit for it. It is those who have sinful natures who can engage in it. And is there one of us to whom this does not apply? The Bible tells us that we "all have sinned and come short of the glory of God." It is those who are burdened with sorrow and sin who are fit for it; for Jesus says, "Come unto Me, all ye that labour and are heavy laden, and I will give you rest." It is those who are in danger of losing their souls who are fit for engaging in this business. And we are all in this danger till we learn to love and serve God. Jesus said, "He that believeth not is condemned already." Now, you know that a *condemned* man is one who has been found guilty of some crime, and who has been sentenced to be executed, and is only waiting for the appointed time to come when he will be led out and put to death. And this is our condition until we truly repent and become Christians by exercising faith in Jesus. We have been found guilty of breaking God's holy law. We are condemned already to everlasting punishment. And if death, the great executioner, should come to us while we are in this state, we are lost for ever. This shows how fit we all are to engage in the business of which we are speaking. But the help of God's Holy Spirit is necessary to fit us for entering upon this business: and can we all get this help? Read Luke xi. 11-13 for an answer. Here Jesus tells us that God is more ready to give the Holy Spirit to them that ask it than parents are to give bread to their children.

The merchandise of wisdom is a business, then, in

ROOM FOR ALL.

which we are all fitted to engage. And we are not only all *fitted*, but all invited to engage in it. "Wisdom crieth at the gates, at the entry of the city, at the coming in at the doors: Unto you, O men, I call; and my voice is to the sons of men. Now, therefore, hearken unto me, O ye children; for blessed are they that keep my ways." Yes, we all have sins enough to fit us to begin the merchandise of wisdom; and God has grace enough to enable us all to go on with it when it is begun. There is room for us all here. There is room in the Church for us to enter. There is room in the world for us to trade in wisdom's treasures; and there is room in heaven, my dear children, for us all to enjoy the everlasting gains of this heavenly merchandise. Jesus said, "Seek ye *first* the kingdom of God and His righteousness, and all other things shall be added unto you." And may God incline you all, my dear children, to begin now to trade in this merchandise, and make you skilful and successful traders, for Jesus' sake! Amen.

THE LESSONS JESUS TEACHES.

"Learn of Me."—MATT. xi. 29.

THIS is a short text. There are only three words in it. But it is a very important text. Do you know, my dear children, who spoke these words? Jesus spoke them. Now, what do we call the person from whom we learn anything? We call him our *teacher*. Then, in what character does Jesus here come before us? As a *Teacher*. It is a great thing to have a good teacher. If the Governor of the State, or the President of the United States, should have a class in Sunday school, the boys who were in his class would feel themselves honoured to have such a teacher. It is said that Queen Victoria of England, when at home in her beautiful palace at Windsor, at one time, had a Sunday school, in which she attended and taught a class of children. If this is so, it reflects great honour upon her. And I suppose the children of her class felt it to be a great privilege to have the queen of that great and mighty nation for their teacher. But, my dear children, what is any earthly governor, or president, or king, or queen, compared with Jesus? Jesus is the Maker and Ruler of the world. He is the Maker and Ruler of all worlds. He is the greatest and best Teacher that ever was. His *position* makes Him great. He sits at the right hand of the throne of God. His *power* makes Him great. "All power in heaven and on earth is given unto Him." He can do whatever He pleases.

His *wisdom* makes Him great. He knows all about everybody who is living now, and everybody who ever has lived. He knows all about everything that ever has taken place, or ever will take place. Oh, He is a great Teacher! What a happy and glorious thing it must be to be *His* scholars! Yet this is just what He wishes *us* to be. In our text we have His invitation to us to enter His school and join His class, and have Him for our Teacher:—" Learn of Me." This is what Jesus says to us all. Now, when we go to school to any person, we wish to know what it is that he will teach us, or what lessons we shall have to learn. And if we have Jesus for our Teacher, we may very well ask what it is that He will teach us. He will teach us *four* things, which it is of the utmost importance for us to learn; but which we never shall learn at all unless He become our teacher. The difference between earthly teachers is not that some teach things which others do not, but it is that some teach them better than others. But the difference between Jesus and other teachers is, not only that He teaches better than others, but that He teaches things which nobody else can teach at all; and which we must for ever remain ignorant of unless we learn them from Him.

Now, let us see what these things are.

And, in the first place, Jesus will teach us to KNOW GOD.

The Bible is the lesson-book which Jesus has prepared for His scholars. It is His *first* lesson-book—His book for beginners. It contains the simplest lessons we can learn on this subject—the very A B C of the knowledge of God. And it contains not only the alphabet of this knowledge, but many higher lessons also on the same subject. All that we can learn about God in this world is contained in the Bible. And if it were not for the Bible and what it has taught us we should know nothing at all about God for certain. Almost everything else men can study and find out by themselves. But however long or hard they might study by themselves, they would never find out anything about God. This is the meaning of that question which is asked in the Bible: "Canst thou by searching find out God? Canst thou find out the Almighty unto perfection? It is high as heaven: what canst thou do? It is deeper than hell: what canst thou know?"

There was a heathen king once who had no Bible, but who wanted to know something about God. It happened so that a very celebrated philosopher, and the wisest man then living, was in this king's dominions. So the king sent for the philosopher and told him he wanted an answer to this question: *What is God?* The philosopher said that this was a very difficult and important question, and he wanted three days' time to consider about it before he attempted to give an answer to it. When the three days were up, he came to the king and asked for five days more. When the five were up, he came again and asked for ten; and when the ten were passed, he came again and told the king that he could not answer his question; for the longer he thought upon the subject the less able he was to say anything about it. And if we were left to ourselves we should know no more about God than this philosopher did. And if Jesus had not come to teach us we never should have known any more. Suppose that you were in a dark room which had a great many pictures hung round on the wall, and you were asked to find out what those pictures were about: could you do it? No. You might strain your eyes ever so much in trying to see through the gloom. You might grope your way in the dark and go feeling round among the pictures. But your fingers would be unable to detect the forms and figures painted there. You never could tell what those pictures were so long as you were left in the dark. And what is it you would want to enable you to know the character of those pictures? Light; yes, light is what you would need. Only let a window be opened in that dark room, and the blessed beams of the sun come pouring in around you, and *then* you could see the pictures and tell in a moment what they were. And this is just our position, without the teachings of the Bible, in reference to God. The world we live in is like a dark room. The glorious works of God that surround us are like pictures of Him hung round the walls of this room. But they are hanging in the dark; and we strive in vain to tell what it is which these pictures represent to us of God. But Jesus has opened a window and let in the light. He is *Himself* that light. St John said of Him, " He is the true Light, which lighteth every man that cometh into the world." Jesus said of Himself, " I am the *Light* of the world." He came into the world on purpose to teach us about God. And this is what Jesus meant when He said, " No man knoweth the Father save the Son, and he to whom the Son doth reveal Him." " No man hath seen God at any time; the only-begotten Son, who is in the bosom of the Father, He hath revealed Him." We know nothing at all of God but what Jesus has taught us. The Bible is full of His teachings. It is the lesson-book He puts into our hands.

But there is a second lesson to speak of: Jesus teaches us to LOVE GOD.

There are different ways of teaching a thing. Deaf people, who cannot hear, are taught by signs. Blind people, who cannot see, are taught by feeling. But even people who are neither blind nor deaf, and who can both see and hear, are taught in different ways. Sometimes people are taught things by studying text-books, which tell all about what they want to learn. Sometimes they are taught by lectures, and sometimes by conversation. But there is only *one* way in which Jesus teaches us to love God. And what is this? Is it by showing us the *power* of God? Does He teach us

> " To sing the almighty power of God,
> Which made the mountains rise,
> Which spread the flowing seas abroad,
> And built the lofty skies,"

in order that we may be led to love Him? No, my dear children; the mere possession of *power* will never excite love.

Is it by showing us the *wisdom* of God? Does He point us to all the marvellous things He has made—the birds with their sweet songs and beautifully-coloured feathers; the insects with their curious contrivances; the trees with their graceful forms; and the fragrant flowers with their hues of varying loveliness? No; this is not the way. If we find out that a person is very wise, we may admire him for his wisdom, but we never should love him for it.

Well, is it by showing us the *riches* of God? Does He point to all the mines of gold and silver, all the treasures of gems and jewels that are in the world, and tell us that they belong to God? Does He show us that "all the beasts of the forest are His, and so are the cattle upon a thousand hills," and ask us to love God because He is so rich? No; this is not the way. Nobody was ever *loved* because he was rich. A great many people love money very much indeed. And people will often serve one another, they will live with one another, and even sometimes marry one another, because they have money; but nobody ever *loved* another because he had money.

It is not in any of these ways that Jesus teaches us to love God. Then how is it? In what way does He do it? Now, mark what I say. *Jesus teaches us to love God by showing us that God loves us.* The surest way in the world to get other persons to love us is to show that we love them. This is the meaning of that old saying, "Love, if you would be loved again." Dr Doddridge, a celebrated minister in England, had a sweet, lovely daughter, who was a great favourite with all the persons who visited at her father's house. One day a gentleman who was there said to her, "Mary, my dear child, tell me what it is that makes everybody love you so." "Indeed, sir," said Mary, "I don't know, unless it is *because I love everybody.*"

But that was just the secret of it.

It is in this way that Jesus teaches us to love God. He proves that God loves us. How does He prove it? Turn

THE LOVE AND SERVICE OF GOD.

to the sixteenth verse of the third chapter of St John's Gospel, and there you will find the proof. It is in these wonderful words: "God so loved the world that He gave His only-begotten Son, that whosoever believeth on Him should not perish, but have everlasting life." Jesus came down from heaven to prove that God loves us. And when He took our nature upon Him, and was born a feeble infant, and was laid in the manger; when He lived a life of poverty and suffering; when He passed through the dreadful agony endured in the Garden of Gethsemane; when He was taken by wicked men, and mocked, and scourged, and crowned with thorns, and nailed to the shameful tree; when He suffered, and groaned, and died, and was laid in the grave,—He was all the time proving to us how much God loves us. And this is the reason why preaching the Gospel to people, and telling them about Jesus, leads them to love God when nothing else will do it. *Jesus teaches us to love God.* This is His second lesson.

But there is a third lesson we are to speak of; and that is, that Jesus teaches us to SERVE GOD.

Now, people make a great many mistakes about the way in which they can serve God. Jesus said that the time would come when men would persecute and kill His people, and think they were doing God service. And this has often been done. The Church of Rome used to have a place called "The Inquisition," which was a horrible kind of prison to which the priests would send people who would not believe just whatever they choose to teach. In that prison they would put people in chains and in dungeons; they would beat them and burn them, and torture them in a great variety of cruel ways, and think that *this* was serving God.

Some people think that serving God means to be honest and industrious, and mind your own business. Some think it means to be kind to the poor. And some think that if they only read the Bible every day, and go to church every Sunday, they are certainly serving God. But people may do all these things and yet never serve God at all.

And if you ask what is the knowledge Jesus gives us about serving God, I answer He shows us in the Gospel that we must repent of our sins, and believe in Him as our Saviour; that is, we must become true Christians. Nobody can begin to serve God aright until their hearts are changed. Whatever we may do, until this takes place we cannot please God. But can we change our own hearts? No; we can no more do this than we can fly. Then where is the power to come from that will change our evil hearts and make us Christians? It can only come from Jesus. His *grace* can do it. Without Him we can do nothing. But with His help we can do all things. And thus it is, my dear children, that the *knowledge* and *power* to serve God come from Jesus. If we want to be the servants of God, then we must *learn of Jesus*. Earthly teachers can often give their scholars knowledge, without being able to give them power. They can show them what to do, but they cannot help them to do it. But Jesus can do both these things. He can give to all who learn of Him both the knowledge and the power that they need. What a blessed thing it is to have such a Teacher! How anxious we should all be to learn of Jesus! *He can teach us to serve God.*

And then there is one lesson more which Jesus can teach us. He can teach us to ENJOY GOD.

My dear children, do you know where all the water which supplies the springs, and fountains, and rills, and rivers of the world comes from? It comes from the ocean. The sun makes it rise from the surface of the ocean in a sort of steam or vapour. The vapour floats away in the sky and forms clouds, and when the clouds are full they empty themselves in rain, and the rain supplies all the springs and fountains.

The ocean, then, is the grand reservoir from which all the water in the world is obtained. There is more water in the ocean than in all the rest of the world put together;

GOD THE SOURCE OF HAPPINESS.

and there is no water in the world but what comes from the ocean. And what the ocean is to the world in regard to the supply of water, God is to the world in regard to its supply of happiness. God is the great ocean of happiness, from which all the fountains, or sources of happiness are supplied. All the real happiness which any of God's creatures experience comes from Him. And there is more happiness in God than in all the rest of the world, or of the universe put together.

Now, seeing this is true, you may well say, "What a wonder it is that all people do not come to God in order to enjoy Him and be happy!" It *is* a wonder. But the reason of it is that people do not know or believe that there is so much happiness in God. They need some one to show them this. And no one can teach us this but Jesus. We have a striking illustration of what I am now speaking of in the history of Hagar in the wilderness. You can read the account of it in the twenty-first chapter of Genesis. Hagar was wandering in the wilderness with her son Ishmael. The water she had carried with her was all gone. They were parched with thirst, and her child was likely to die. She was in great distress. She laid her child down under a bush, and turned away from him and wept. While she was weeping the angel of the Lord came and showed her a well of water. Then she was glad, and drank from the well, and gave her son as much water as he wanted. You see, my dear children, it does not say that the angel *made* a well of water. He did not strike the rock, as Moses did afterwards, and make the water gush out. He only *showed* her the well. It was there before, and probably not far off; but she did not see it. She needed some one to show her the well. And just so it is with us. We need happiness, but know not where to find it. God is a well-spring of never-failing happiness. And "He is not far from every one of us." Still, we need some one to act the part of this good angel, and show us where the well is. We need some one to teach us how to find our enjoyment and happiness in God. And this is what Jesus is able and willing to do for us. This is one thing that He means when He says, "*Learn of Me.*" And if we do learn of Him He will make us really happy. He said, on one occasion, "Whoso drinketh of the water that I shall give him shall never thirst: but the water that I shall give him shall be in him a well of water, springing up into everlasting life." Those whom Jesus teaches to enjoy God are the happiest persons alive. They have more happiness in *this* life than any other persons; while nobody can describe the happiness prepared for them in the life to come. Surely, my dear children, these are the most valuable lessons we can ever learn. Nobody in the world can teach them to us but Jesus. Then let us come and *learn of Him.* If we want to *know* God, let us learn of Jesus. If we want to *love* God, let us learn of Jesus. If we want to *serve* God, let us learn of Jesus. And if we want to *enjoy* God, let us learn of Jesus.

Jesus is the best of all teachers, and the knowledge which He gives is the best of all knowledge. The apostle Paul was a very learned man. He had been taught by one of the most famous teachers in the world at that day. But when Paul became a Christian, and began to learn of Jesus, he thought the knowledge which He gives so excellent that all the other knowledge he had gained was good for nothing in comparison with it. And Paul was right. And the knowledge of Christ Jesus our Lord is just as excellent and valuable to us as it was to him. Then let us all begin at once to learn of Jesus, and He will make us wise unto salvation. Remember, my dear children, that this is the message of Jesus to you. He says to each one of you, "LEARN OF ME."

THE END.

www.ingramcontent.com/pod-product-compliance
Lightning Source LLC
Chambersburg PA
CBHW062223080426
42734CB00010B/2007